MW00623967

JAMES W. WHITEHEAD

A FRAGILE UNION

The Story of Louise Herreshoff

Second edition

Copyright © 2003, 2006 by James W. Whitehead

Library of Congress No. TXu-1-091-968
United States Copyright Office

ISBN 0-9777220-0-7

All rights reserved, including the right of reproduction
in whole or in part in any form.

Herreshoff paintings and
Photographs of porcelain from the Reeves Collection
courtesy of the Reeves Center,
Washington and Lee University, Lexington, Virginia

Designed by Communication Design, Inc., Richmond, Virginia

Produced by Business Publications Inc., New York, New York

Published by Celeste Dervaes Whitehead

I dedicate this story to
Elisabeth Shelton Gottwald
and
Floyd Dewey Gottwald, Jr.

Without their boundless generosity and
unflagging commitment, the Reeves Center at
Washington and Lee University
never would have evolved as a study center
of ceramics for students and scholars and
as a showcase for the Louise Herreshoff paintings.

Their friendship to the students and staff
of the Reeves Center will ever be
an encouragement and inspiration.

CONTENTS

FOREWORD

BY TOM WOLFE

Dickens would have gladly died and gone to Heaven if only he could have written the story awaiting us in the pages that follow. Dickens' stock in trade was the child who grows up orphaned in a callous world, such as Pip in *Great Expectations*, the little boy we meet in the novel's famous first chapter in a graveyard at twilight whimpering over the tombstones of his father and his mother and his five brothers who died in infancy. The heroine of *A Fragile Union*, our little Louise, out-Pips Pip right down to the last detail. She has been orphaned not merely by death but also by an insidious piece of moral extortion that does not come to light for decades. À la Pip, we meet Louise in the first chapter bereft before a tomb at night . . . in a graveyard scene, the first of many, in fact, compared to which Pip's is the annual flower drop at the cemetery after Easter service.

Believe me, Dickens would not have been the only great writer to eat his heart out over *A Fragile Union*. If Edith Wharton could have dreamed up the story herein, she would have been rendered spastic by a eureakish euphoria on the one hand (I've *found* it!) and on the other, fear, two kinds of it. Would even *her* surpassing talent be equal to the telling of so rich and Byzantine a tale? And how about her readers? They

were liable to think she'd gone hog wild with hubris and manufactured a story so implausible, it insulted their intelligence.

Mrs. Wharton's stock in trade — incidentally, having read her treatise on decor and decorum, *The Decoration of Houses*, I can't imagine calling her simply "Wharton," which sounds like somebody's butler — Mrs. Wharton's stock in trade was the young woman in the ineffable first bloom of youth, or the admirable young man in the season of the rising sap, who is walled off forever from the mate that fate had me created for . . . by society's rigid conventions or the disapproval of parents and other meddlers. I vastly admire Mrs. Wharton's portraits of thwarted young souls with unslaked sexual longings. But what are Charity Royall, Countess Olenska, Newland Archer and Ethan Frome, unforgettable as they are, compared to the heroine we are about to meet? Our little Louise is denied Life's One Great Love not once but three times. Her guardians and elders find no deceit too despicable or too petty. They intercept Mr. Life's One Great Love's love letters to her and throw them down the memory hole. They pack her off to Europe on false pretexts to keep her away from him. They go so far, and so low, as to switch place cards at a dinner to keep him from her side for even a few hours in a room full of starchly proper people. He ends up marrying a young woman he meets at the other end of the table. I don't want to give away any more of the plot, for this book's suspense is too beautifully crafted to be trifled with; but we are also about to see Love Finally Found, found in a way the bards and balladeers, the Shakespeares, Shelleys, Schillers, Scheherezades, Shirelles and Shanahnahs have never sung of.

Moreover, our story has a power no novel or poem can match. Which is to say, little Louise's saga is entirely true. That, I promise you, is an enormous advantage. I wrote nonfiction for twenty years before writing my first novel. I quickly learned that the problem with fiction is that it has to be plausible. Life doesn't — and, in an age like ours, chronically, epidemically, pandemically, gloriously, notoriously and uproariously isn't.

Louise Herreshoff Eaton Reeves' life was implausible and real, all too real. She was born in 1876 to John Brown Francis Herreshoff, socially luminous great-grandson of Rhode Island's legendary eighteenth-century shipping mogul, John Brown, and Grace Dyer of the not-quite-so-grand-but-grand-enough Dyers who in the seventeenth century had fought the Indians on the frontier. Little Louise's mother died when she was four, but her upbringing was as proper as Providence, Rhode Island, and Herreshoff money could make it. Like Mrs. Wharton, who had been born fourteen years earlier, Louise was on the face of it the typical young woman of the American leisure class who took the Grand Tour of Europe, for cultivation. Little Louise went to Paris as an art student and studied at the renowned Académie Julian. She proved to be no mere Grand Tour dilet-tante. In 1900, when she was twenty-three, one of her paint-ings was selected for the Paris Salon's annual exhibition and another for the New York National Academy's, certifying her as a serious contender in the world of art. In 1903 the Paris exhibition chose one of her greatest works, *Girl in Garden*. In 1927, as we shall see, she abruptly gave up painting. This, the public side of her life, soon sank without a bubble to the bot-tom of a lake of amnesia, along with her personal history.

T he man we have to thank for retrieving both is our nar-rator, James W. Whitehead. I ran into Jim Whitehead when he was curator of my alma mater Washington and Lee's huge new collection of Chinese Export porcelain, an esoteric antique genre I had never heard of, to be perfectly honest. Jim Whitehead's place in the larger cosmos, however, couldn't have been more instantly comprehensible. His clothes lay lovingly tailored upon his well-fed-and-cared-for contours. His cravats would have made England's legendary cravateur, Beau Brummel, twitch with envy. He had a peculiarly Southern courtesy and conversational ease and a Columbus, Georgia, voice that could have charmed the Rolex off your wrist, had he entertained any such prospects. I hasten to add that he didn't. If Washington and Lee, which placed a great emphasis on the flawless gentlemen, had wanted to send out into the world a logo personality, on the order of Chuck Yeager for Delco, Michael Jordan for Nike, Jamie Lee Curtis for Verizon, Alastair Cook for PBS, to rally lively and cultivated folk everywhere around the university, they would have launched James W. Whitehead worldwide in a flash.

He would have some notable glamour available for the ride. In 1938 he had met his bride-to-be, a fellow student at the University of Tampa, a gorgeous adventuress named Celeste Dervaes who volunteered for a World War II college program to train civilian pilots and became the first woman trainee in the South to solo. He took his cue from her, volunteered for the Navy, became an aviator and flew in the Pacific until the end of the war. In due course, he became a Washington and Lee administrator, ultimately treasurer — and discoverer of the Reeves Collection, as the porcelain trove was called. Overnight he found himself in the role of curator, archivist, connoisseur, museologist (recent art-world coinage), and impresario. In fact, he turned out to be a born impresario. That was a good thing. Only a born impresario could have marshalled the talent, determination, and enthusiasm — not least of all in the form of the species *donor enthusiasmus* — it took to create that rare

gem amid the junkyard dogs of contemporary museum design, Washington and Lee's Reeves Center.

And now, herewith, between these covers, he establishes himself as an author. How anyone who has never tried it before could create a book with a structure as sophisticated as *A Fragile Union*'s is beyond me.

In the first half he recounts most of little Louise's life, the underhanded way in which she was doomed to be an orphan, her nocturnal visits to the graveyard, the meddlers who denied her A Woman's One Great Love, her triumphs as an artist, and the shock that shuts down her magnificent talent forever. All this Ensign Whitehead (U.S.N.R., Ret.) — as with Mrs. Wharton, it strikes me as a gaffe to refer to someone of James W. Whitehead's eminent gentility as "Whitehead," as if he were a malingering New England boarding school boy about to be whacked across the hand with a ruler in Latin class — all this Ensign Whitehead tells in the third person. He's a cool hand at suspense. The very last sentence of the first half of *A Fragile Union* leaves us in the state of felinecidal curiosity the great serial novelists, Dickens, Dostoyevsky, Thackeray, Zola, Trollope, Daudet, specialized in.

So it comes as a jarring note when Ensign Whitehead opens the second half in his own voice: "I." For two or three paragraphs we seem to be reading nothing more than his museological recollections of how he tracked down Louise Herreshoff Eaton Reeves' china collection. Before we know it, however, we find ourselves in another world, a veritable time capsule of the late-nineteenth-century American Leisure Class's last Gothic gasp ... hidden ... scruffy in the fox stole, scuffed in the spats, shabby in the gentility ... deep within a late-twentieth-century Providence slum. Suspense now builds at a lit-fuse pace. We are with Ensign Whitehead in the here and now as he comes face to face with little Louise herself. She is ancient, bed-ridden, near death . . . but all there . . . and articulate and frank. In the most graphic way imaginable we *see* . . . what in fact had happened next . . . following the tantalizing end of our drama's Act I. In a brilliant denouement, the Ensign himself discovers 120 of little Louise's paintings, frozen in time, buried in dust, the earthly remains of the utterly forgotten triumphs of her youth.

Perhaps I've already revealed too much of the extraordinary story you are about to read, but I can't resist one last note. There comes a moment near the end when one of the four or five reigning experts on nineteenth- and early-twentieth-century American art, a man who never heard of Louise Herreshoff Eaton Reeves until five minutes ago, enters a pitch black room and — *just like that* — before his very eyes a spotlight beam picks out a single object suspended in the darkness, a painting by our little Louise — and he exclaims, "My God!" — and pronounces it as great as the very greatest of turn-of-the-nineteenth-century American art. At that moment you will be more of a Spartan than I am if you don't feel a catch in your throat.

With that, I entrust you to the deft hands of James W. Whitehead.

INTRODUCTION

This account of the life of Louise Herreshoff Reeves is written for the students — past, present and future — of the Reeves Center at Washington and Lee University in Lexington, Virginia. It is also for those who have been inspired and fascinated by the life and life's work of an accomplished painter, tireless collector and generous benefactor. Understanding the period, places and events of her life will, I hope, provide a keener insight into this remarkable woman.

Born Louise Chamberlain Herreshoff on November 29, 1876, in Brooklyn, New York, she would, nonetheless, claim Providence, Rhode Island, as her birthplace. Reared there by a spinster aunt, Elizabeth Hannah Dyer (called alternately and affectionately "Wisam" and "Aunt Lizzie"), Louise would marry Charles Curtis Eaton, a distant cousin, in 1910. Her life with him would be brief. Later she would meet and marry Euchlin Dalcho Reeves Jr., a graduate of the Washington and Lee University School of Law. Through her marriage to Euc Reeves, she would become acquainted with the university.

This story is not intended to be a definitive biography of Louise Herreshoff Reeves. The facts related here I have collected through countless conversations and meetings with members of the Herreshoff and Reeves families, their friends and acquaintances. Memories that were recalled to me may have been logical speculation or vivid imagination. The facts come also from letters, photographs, newspaper clippings; from visits to family homes and burial sites; and from statistical record offices in New York, Rhode Island and Massachusetts as well as the National Archives of the United States and France. These were the milestones along a beautiful and exciting odyssey to discover Louise.

The extraordinary histories of Louise's ancestors, the families of John Brown of Rhode Island, William Dyer of Maine, and Karl Frederich Herreschoff (né Herr Eschoff) of Prussia and their descendants in the eighteenth, nineteenth and twentieth centuries have been documented in various books, biographies, journals, magazines and newspaper articles in the United States and Europe.

Louise's paternal ancestor, Herr Karl Frederich Eschoff, was born in Minden in Prussia and schooled with the nobility under the auspices of Frederick the Great. Fathered by a member of the king's elite guard, Eschoff, who later changed his name to Herreschoff, was raised in the Sans Souci Palace in Potsdam, spoke several languages and, to the king's great delight, developed into an able flutist. In 1791 he emigrated to New York and joined John Brown's flourishing trade shipping business. After pursuing Brown's daughter Sarah for several years, he won her hand in 1801.

Each subsequent generation of the Brown–Herreshoff union found new skills and directions for their talents. Marine design, chemical and political science, mechanical engineering, higher education, music and art are all woven into Louise's ancestry. Three generations later, as the only child of J. B. Francis Herreshoff and Grace Eugenia Dyer, Louise, too, would find her own talent and follow in the Brown–Herreshoff tradition.

The Victorian influences of her early years in Providence and New York and the freedom she found in Europe at the turn of the twentieth century would mold her world until midlife. The last quarter of the nineteenth century and the first quarter of the twentieth century, before and after her short-lived marriage, were spent with her beloved aunt.

At the death of Aunt Lizzie, divorced from Charles Eaton and alone, Louise's life abruptly changed and, for a while, she withdrew from society. Later she would meet Euchlin D. Reeves Jr. and their shared mutual interests led to marriage — and to this story.

Dramatic change in both occurred over their years together, and the result would eventually shape their legacy. Euchlin entered Louise's world quite late but would play one of the most important roles. Louise and Euchlin, following earlier interests, became ardent, knowledgeable and dedicated collectors. Beautiful and delicate porcelain determined her pursuit, and items of American history directed his. Often their two goals would combine.

Shortly after her husband's death, Mrs. Reeves bestowed upon Washington and Lee University their treasures of seventeenth-, eighteenth- and nineteenth-century objects of art amassed during their lives. Two hundred barrels and cartons of ceramics — between 3,000 and 4,000 pieces — together with miscellaneous works of art and 103 pieces of antique furniture were given to the university.

The Reeves Center, on the university's National Historic Landmark front campus, now houses tangible links to the period of the founding of the peripatetic institution in 1749 as Augusta Academy. The small school became Liberty Hall Academy in 1776, prior to the signing of the Declaration of Independence. George Washington's gift of James River Canal stock in 1796 ensured the survival of the Academy and again the name was changed. The school became Washington Academy and a few years later, Washington College. Following the leadership of General Robert E. Lee as president of the College, the Board of Trustees in 1871 named the institution Washington and Lee University.

Shards of eighteenth-century English soft-paste porcelain, pottery and fragile Chinese porcelain used by the students and teachers of Liberty Hall Academy were unearthed in the early 1970s during an archaeological dig, directed by Professor John M. McDaniel, at the stone ruins on the site of the early school. Students found hundreds of ceramic bits and pieces exactly matching items in the Reeves Collection. English creamware, pearlware, featheredge, softpaste, Chinese and German hard-paste porcelain and Chinoiserie became new additions to students' vocabulary.

Nearly a half-century later, the Reeves Center of Washington and Lee University stands uniquely among colleges and universities as a study and research collection of ceramics and paintings.

To have known Euchlin Reeves for three years and Louise Herreshoff Reeves for four months was a rare privilege. My major regret in retrospect will always be the many questions that I should have asked during the time of our association. But I knew not what to ask. For me it was a new world, entered into by accident, following the receipt at the university of a penny postcard.

Setting this remembrance to paper started in earnest then — more than forty years ago. For the last decade and a half, I have benefited greatly from the able and patient assistance of Hunter Applewhite, a Washington and Lee alumnus, friend and former Reeves Center volunteer. From Mount Auburn to Providence to Philadelphia, New York, London and Paris, together he, Celeste and I retraced Louise's story. Throughout, he never failed to summon the perfect word or

faultless phrase; his help was indispensable in navigating the often choppy waters of writing, designing and printing this book.

And now, as I close the door of 93 Benevolent Street, the interior light fades and darkness moves throughout the old house, which waits unwillingly to serve new masters. How grateful I am to have Tom Wolfe, a titan of American letters, at my side to turn the key and secure each lock. Could the Reeveses or I have asked for more?

— J.W.W.
Lynchburg, Virginia
September 2003

LOUISE HERRESHOFF'S FAMILY TREE

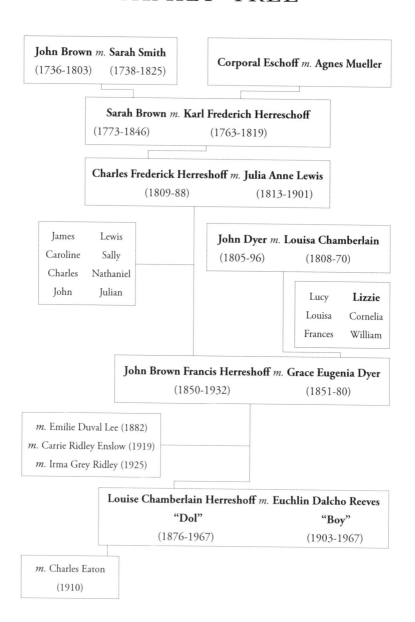

John Brown *m.* **Sarah Smith**
(1736-1803)   (1738-1825)

Corporal Eschoff *m.* **Agnes Mueller**

Sarah Brown *m.* **Karl Frederich Herreschoff**
(1773-1846)   (1763-1819)

Charles Frederick Herreshoff *m.* **Julia Anne Lewis**
(1809-88)   (1813-1901)

James   Lewis
Caroline   Sally
Charles   Nathaniel
John   Julian

John Dyer *m.* **Louisa Chamberlain**
(1805-96)   (1808-70)

Lucy   **Lizzie**
Louisa   Cornelia
Frances   William

John Brown Francis Herreshoff *m.* **Grace Eugenia Dyer**
(1850-1932)   (1851-80)

m. Emilie Duval Lee (1882)
m. Carrie Ridley Enslow (1919)
m. Irma Grey Ridley (1925)

Louise Chamberlain Herreshoff *m.* **Euchlin Dalcho Reeves**
"Dol"   "Boy"
(1876-1967)   (1903-1967)

m. Charles Eaton
(1910)

A FRAGILE UNION

The Story of Louise Herreshoff

CHAPTER

1

THE MAUSOLEUM

The gray metal padlock, pock-marked and pitted from exposure to the cold and damp of New England's coastal climate, was fused to the latch on the heavy steel door. It alone protected the caskets within the family mausoleum. Each year the lock became more obstinate in its refusal to be opened. Now, in 1927, for the ninth time in eighty-one years, it would be unlocked.

On April 23 of that year, the *Providence Journal* carried this obituary:

> Miss Elizabeth Dyer Dead in Her 88th Year
> Member of Old Providence Family Survived
> By Sister and Niece
>
> Miss Elizabeth H. Dyer of 11 Charles Field Street, member of an old distinguished East Side family, died yesterday in her 88th year. Miss Dyer had been living with her sister Miss Helen Cornelia Dyer who survives her, in virtual retirement from society for a number of years. She leaves a niece Mrs. Louise Herreshoff Eaton of the Bristol Herreshoff family and a prominent member of the Providence Art Club. Internment at Mount Auburn Cemetery, Cambridge, Massachusetts.

In late May, following Lizzie's entombment, her surviving sister, Helen Cornelia Dyer, wrote Mount Auburn Cemetery on Louise Eaton's behalf.

MOUNT AUBURN CEMETERY, CAMBRIDGE, MASSACHUSETTS, C. 1847
(ENGRAVING BY JAMES SMILLIE)

Providence, May 22/27
The Superintendent
Mount Auburn Cemetery

When my sister Elizabeth Hannah Dyer was buried five weeks ago — in our tomb marked JOHN DYER on Willow Avenue, Mr. Knowles our undertaker told us the casket was iron and ingot with glass plate screwed down very tight, so we might go to the tomb and have it opened and see Miss Dyer. Now my niece Mrs. Eaton agreed with Mr. Knowles that she should come to Mount Auburn sometime and open the casket. The glass plate is screwed down very tight and Mr. Knowles said it would be all right to lift the cover.

Now we want to know when we set the date if you will have a man there to see if the screws need to be tightened after riding so far as the riding might have loosened them, also will you have the tomb opened when we set the date and I will send you the blue paper which is a guarantee that the tomb belongs to us.

Please answer and tell me if you will have a man there to open the casket after the tomb is open.

Very truly yours,
Helen Cornelia Dyer

John Peterson, Mount Auburn's superintendent, was quick to reply. "A body once being buried is never disturbed," he wrote, "except by order of the Board of Health, the Medical Examiner or the State authorities for some legal reason that necessitates such action."

The illegality of her surviving aunt's request did not deter Louise. She proceeded as petitioned without the superintendent's knowledge. For a two-dollar stipend, she found a willing groundsman to assist her at twilight. Faithfully with the change of each season following Elizabeth Dyer's death, Louise Herreshoff Eaton traveled alone from Providence, Rhode Island, to Mount Auburn Cemetery, near the banks of the Charles River in Cambridge, Massachusetts. Once there, she would unlock the steel door and, with the help of her

"Wisam," Louise's Aunt Lizzie Dyer,
with the lace handkerchief, about 1860

accomplice from the grounds crew, pry open the top of the heavy iron casket. Sitting motionless on a marble bench, Louise would stare almost entranced through a glass enclosure at the embalmed body of Elizabeth Dyer, her Aunt Lizzie, whom she had called Wisam.

Spring sunlight filtered through the reticulated door into the vault in April; summer heat in July dried the dampness; falling leaves in October made shadows dance along the wall and caskets. Winter returned the tomb to cold bleakness.

In December 1928, in a private burial ceremony and with no sign of emotion on Louise's part, Aunt Cornelia joined her parents, brother, four younger sisters and Lizzie as the Dyer vault's tenth and last occupant. The crypt had reached its capacity.

Louise's ritual visits to the Dyer vault continued until her early fears proved prophetic. The long ride of the hearse from Providence to Cambridge had indeed loosened the screws that anchored the glass cover to the casket. Air and elements had seeped in. Though imperceptible during Louise's earliest visits, slight changes became obvious over time. The linen shroud began to fade and mold itself in the shape of the bones it covered as it sank into each crevice of Lizzie's body. The skin of her face began to fade, discolor and turn brittle, clinging to her high, gaunt cheekbones.

Finally, after more than a year of faithful visits, Louise, alone, loosened the screws, and with great effort, lifted the glass plate. Weeping, she took from her purse a lace handkerchief, Wisam's favorite since school days, and gently placed it over her beloved aunt's face. She lowered the glass cover and the iron lid and never saw her Aunt Lizzie again.

Louise returned to Mount Auburn several times a year but never again opened Lizzie's casket. At the end of each trip, she would place several small stones atop the iron lid to let Wisam know she had been there.

A FRAGILE UNION

JOHN DYER OBELISK, MOUNT AUBURN CEMETERY,
CAMBRIDGE, MASSACHUSETTS

In time the key no longer turned the frozen, rusted cylinder, and Louise's visits inside the dark, dank vault ended. She ordered the crypt completely covered over, buried under tons of soil and planted in grass. Inexplicably, she left uncovered three stone steps that led to the vault's entrance. With it now covered and no longer visible, the steps seemingly led nowhere.

Rising twenty feet above the mound of earth and topped with a carved floral urn, a marble obelisk, commissioned by Louise, identified the family that lay below. The name "John Dyer" was chiseled deep into the granite base. Four side panels carried the names of three generations of Dyers. Infant son William died in 1846, followed by a grandson, John Shaw, in 1865. John Dyer, the patriarch, died in 1896. He was entombed with his wife Louisa. Later, their six daughters, Grace, Frances, Louisa, Lucy, Elizabeth and Cornelia, would join them.

Louise's mother, Grace Dyer Herreshoff, was among those whose caskets lay within. But it was her surrogate mother — Grace's sister Elizabeth, Aunt Lizzie — who inspired Louise to return time and again to the vault.

A large Normandy maple, a tea crabapple tree from China, bayberry shrubs and English ivy marked the Dyers' cemetery plot No. 3341 at the horseshoe bend on Willow Avenue off Poplar Avenue. A rough granite stone, unpolished and without ornamentation, two feet wide by a foot and a half high, was placed on the left side of the uncovered steps. Louise had the name "Louise Herreshoff Eaton" carved into this nondescript marker. With the stone in place, and the entire vault buried, Louise had emotionally interred herself with her beloved Wisam.

The years passed, and Louise's visits to Mount Auburn grew infrequent. The ivy's tentacled leaves completely obscured Louise's stone marker and the vault with its three generations of the Dyer family. Only the three stone steps and the obelisk resisted encroachment.

Early in the first half of the nineteenth century, John Dyer had selected Mount Auburn Cemetery, a short mile from Harvard Square, to be his family's burial site. His wife, Louisa Chamberlain Dyer, born in nearby Boston, had urged the choice. Though residents of Providence, the Dyer family found a certain gracious stability in the social standing that Mount Auburn conferred, even in death.

Consecrated in 1831, Mount Auburn was America's first garden cemetery. The natural beauty of more than 150 acres of undulating terrain, ponds, flowering trees and plants amid sculptures of tribute and remembrance combined to justify its reputation as the most beautiful cemetery in the East. In time it became the final resting place for many distinguished Americans: Oliver Wendell Holmes, Winslow Homer, Julia Ward Howe, Henry Wadsworth Longfellow, Edwin Booth, Henry Lodge, Mary Baker Eddy, Amy Lowell and James Russell Lowell were all interred among its 65,000 graves.

In nineteenth-century New England, it was vital to maintain the status of acceptance, once achieved — certainly so for the Dyers. Victorian manners and mores strictly dictated religious, political and social behavior. Without exception, black was worn as an outward display of mourning and respect for a deceased family member, both close and distant. Few seasons passed when the somber color and respect for the dead were not in evidence.

It was in this atmosphere of pious gloom that Louise spent a major part of her life, from the age of four and the death of her mother Grace. It was a life directed and dominated with love and obsession by her maiden Aunt Lizzie. Two other spinster aunts in the household, Lucy and Cornelia, vied for Louise's affection, but Lizzie's protective shield prevented any other close attachments.

The maternal role came naturally to the efficient and strong-willed Lizzie, as she became her father John Dyer's main support in 1870 at the death of his wife Louisa. She would handle the details connected with the funeral service and burial of her mother at Mount Auburn. Six years later, she would find herself in a mother's role as she arranged the last wedding of her family's generation.

◆

In 1876, Grace Elizabeth, the youngest of the six Dyer sisters, became engaged to John Brown Francis Herreshoff, son of Carl Frederick and Sarah Lewis Herreshoff of Bristol, Rhode Island, on Narragansett Bay.

Frank, as the prospective groom was called, was one of nine children. He completed his education at Brown University in the 1870s and, while a chemistry student there, was named a laboratory assistant and later joined the faculty. The university had been named for his great-grandfather John Brown and John's three brothers, Nicholas, Joseph and Moses. In 1770 the Brown brothers succeeded in having Rhode Island College, founded six years earlier, locate in Providence, rather than Newport. It was renamed Brown University in 1804 to recognize the benefactors, who were among Rhode Island's most distinguished families.

The renaming also recognized John Brown's early leadership in America's struggle for independence from British crown. Brown won early patriotic fame in 1772 for attacking the British tax vessel *Gaspee* eighteen months before the more famous Boston Tea Party. The armed schooner had run aground after entering Narragansett Bay. Brown, with a small party of volunteers, overpowered the crew and set the

PORTRAIT OF GEORGE WASHINGTON,
ATTRIBUTED TO GILBERT STUART,
GIVEN TO THE BENGALI MERCHANT RAMDOOLAL DEY IN 1803

Gaspee afire. It was the first major open rebellion against King George III.

John Brown prospered during the early years of independence. Ships he owned with his brother Nicholas plied the China and India trade routes. From Canton, Calcutta and other exotic East Indian ports, his trading company brought to New England the fruits of the Far East: teas, spices, silks and porcelain.

Although America had won its freedom, many of these Far Eastern ports were still dominated by the British. In Calcutta, a Hindu merchant named Ramdoolal Dey, who had risen from abject poverty to become one of India's wealthiest traders, befriended American seamen. In gratitude, the captains gave him an oil portrait of their country's greatest hero, George Washington. Ramdoolal Dey proudly hung the portrait of Washington, attributed to the noted American artist Gilbert Stuart, in his Calcutta home. Almost two centuries later, the portrait would return to America, thanks to an admirer of the legacy of John Brown's great-great-granddaughter.

In 1786, Brown began construction on a home that would properly reflect his growing wealth and stature as a Providence merchant, enriched by numerous commercial ventures. His brother Joseph designed the brick mansion on Power and Benefit Streets; it featured a stunning central staircase of mahogany wood brought from Santo Domingo at Brown's specific request. John Quincy Adams is said to have considered it the grandest house in the new nation.

President George Washington stayed with John Brown on his visits to Providence. Brown was a great admirer and named three of his ships for the revolutionary patriot, soldier and statesman: the *Washington,* the *General Washington* and the *President Washington.*

While the Browns were helping establish Providence in the early seventeenth century, members of the Dyer family

CHINESE EXPORT PORCELAIN MADE FOR THE AMERICAN MARKET,
ABOUT 1794, FROM THE REEVES COLLECTION

were defending themselves from Indian attacks farther up the coast in Dyer's Neck, Maine. Several of John Dyer's ancestors were massacred in open daylight as they tended their crops. A sworn deposition, entered in 1738, described the hardship:

> I lived with my grandfather William Dyer on a Certain Neck of Land near the Old Town of Sheepscott in the County of Cornwall, which Neck of Land was called Nassoemek by the Indians, and Dyer's Neck by the English. A War with the Indians breaking out in 1689, my grandfather was killed by them in August and in December following, my father Christopher was killed.

The deposition further stated that the land had been purchased for a reasonable consideration by William Dyer Sr., Esq., from "Two of the Indians Sachems, named Robin Hood & Daniel Sagamore." On this land William Dyer built a house, raised a family, tilled his garden, planted an orchard and cared for his cattle. Both he and his son Christopher would be killed by Indians. Louise's grandfather, John Dyer of Providence, was a direct descendent. The Brown and Dyer families experienced in different ways the hardships and the struggles as a new nation gained independence through toil and armed revolution to establish the American republic.

It was a hundred years later, in February 1876, that Grace Elizabeth Dyer and John Brown Francis Herreshoff would be married after a twelve-month courtship. Louise Chamberlain Herreshoff, their only child, was born nine months later.

It was this child, Louise, grown to womanhood, who would spend each day next to Aunt Lizzie's bed as she lay dying, recording on small slips of paper every word her aunt uttered, rational or irrational. The dominant force that guided Louise for more than fifty years was fading away. Who would now direct her every move?

Lizzie, by then in her late eighties, had enjoyed a remarkably healthy life that enabled her to care for her father and her unmarried sisters over the years. But as life ebbed, suffering from pneumonia, Lizzie only murmured or sometimes cried out:"The cold, it's so taxing . . . The roses they're coals of fire . . . The days are not half long enough . . . Hold on to the pennies, and the dollars will take care of themselves . . . It's a long road that has no turning . . . I want to grow old gracefully . . . I feel bad all through me . . . Why? Why? . . ." Words of guidance and love — the words Louise wished to hear — never came.

Following strict instructions given before her death, Aunt Lizzie's body was laid in an ingot-iron coffin. A heavy plate-glass inner cover permitted the corpse to be observed when the casket top was open. Lined with a bed of soft satin, Lizzie, in a shroud of delicate cream linen, ruffled high with lace at the neck, lay in repose in the parlor of the Dyer home on Charles Field Street. Family and, by invitation, close friends, all in mourning black, sat beside the open coffin. The famed Boston photographer Louis Fabian Bacharach recorded the scene. Lizzie's face in the picture appears carved in stone, with pink powder slightly softening her features. An outpouring of sympathy letters arrived. Louise opened some and left others sealed.

The remaining Dyer sister, Cornelia, at age eighty-five, could do little to console or comfort her niece Louise. With Lizzie gone, the Dyer home on Charles Field Street was a hollow shell in which each sound seemed to echo its human emptiness. Only the memories of nearly a century remained.

Many of those were best forgotten.

Louise, in severe depression and despair, was unable to accept the loss of Aunt Lizzie. She suffered a nervous breakdown and was admitted to the Butler Sanitarium on the outskirts of Providence. Several months of intense counseling, medication and therapy brought improved health and her return to Charles Field Street. Her regular visits to Mount Auburn Cemetery would soon resume.

To occupy her mind and time further, Louise purchased a small house at 93 Benevolent Street, a few blocks away. She remodeled the frame structure, inside and out. Dark-red brick covered the wooden exterior, with iron bars to protect the downstairs windows. She had the chimneys filled with cement and a coal-burning furnace installed in the basement to supply heat. The areas surrounding the house were paved with brick and stone. A heavy cast iron fence surrounded the yard. To the back of the house, Louise added two small rooms made of heavy stones a foot thick. Entry to the vault was from the back of the dining-room pantry through two steel doors. A metal front door was installed with five Yale safety locks. Louise had conceived, designed and built her own mausoleum.

Aunt Cornelia's death soon after moving with her niece to 93 Benevolent left Louise its solitary occupant, completely alone for the first time in her life. Close friends and relatives of Louise, though few, attempted to fill the void left by the deaths of her two aunts.

Invitations came from her cousins Grace Dyer Knight and Maude Dyer deCamp of Brookline, Massachusetts. They tried to persuade Louise to join them in their travels across the United States and to Europe, but the offers yielded no interest from Louise. She left the cloistered world she had created at 93 Benevolent Street only rarely. Without Wisam to direct, encourage, care for and love her, she was lost. Convinced that no one could or would ever fulfill those needs, Louise at the age of fifty became a recluse.

During the months that followed at 93 Benevolent Street, she slowly began to realize and accept that her life since childhood had been shaped by the self-interest of others, sometimes well-meaning and, at times, otherwise.

A FRAGILE UNION

AUNT LIZZIE AT HER DEATH, 1927

A GLASS COVER WAS PLACED IN HER CASKET
SO LOUISE COULD SEE HER BELOVED WISAM
ON RETURN VISITS TO MOUNT AUBURN CEMETERY

Though isolated, she was not without ample diversions that filled the house at 93 Benevolent when she moved from Charles Field Street: old steamer trunks with faded stickers from seaports around the world, leather valises brittle with age, packing boxes, dresser and bureau drawers which, when opened, spewed forth old newspaper clippings, letters, diaries and photographs of relatives and friends, both remembered and forgotten.

A bedroom on the second floor of 93 Benevolent was furnished exactly as Aunt Lizzie's room had been the night she died at the Dyer home on Charles Field Street. On the outside, untrimmed vines forced their way skyward, through cracks in the cement that surrounded the base of the house, with leaves covering the bedroom's lone window. Inside, Lizzie's own Victorian furniture, an ornate bed and dresser with mirror, a slanted tilt-top desk with a green felt writing surface, a rocking chair with a cushioned seat and back, a bedside table and a caned bottom straight chair sat atop a faded Belgian machine-woven carpet. A number of framed pictures depicted religious scenes; others showed European sites Lizzie had visited with Louise. Brass oil lamps with multicolored glass shades, converted for electric light bulbs, were on the bedside table, desk and dresser.

Directly opposite the dresser on the far wall hung an oil portrait of Lizzie that had been painted shortly before her death.

A large, heavy metal safe contained mourning jewelry with bits of hair preserved inside glass-covered lockets, hair belonging to three generations of Dyers. Carved cameos from Italy, hatpins, strands of pearls from Asia, cuff links and brooches, gold mountings, cut and uncut diamonds, opals and other precious and semi-precious stones also sat in the safe.

Scraps of torn letters and wadded pieces of paper opened new avenues of family history. Fact and lore evoked fleeting joy, extreme sadness and deep hatred.

On each side of the walnut-framed mirror that rested on the dresser's gray-veined marble top were two drawers. Louise never dared open a drawer in Lizzie's dresser or desk in all the years they had lived together on Charles Field Street. Louise hesitated at first and then hurriedly opened the drawer on the right side of the mirror's base. Inside, Lizzie's personal life of nearly nine decades was catalogued through letters, notes and papers bundled together in neat little packages and tied with cotton string. A few were tied with crimson ribbon, nearly colorless with age. Untying the cotton bow that bound a package of ten or more letters, still in envelopes, the fragile paper at times disintegrated between her fingers and the faded ink and pencil were often illegible.

She recognized immediately the handwriting in the first bundle: It was her own. Thumbing through other bundles in the first drawer, Louise remembered writing from Brooklyn, Philadelphia and Paris during her teenage years. Each letter began "Dear Wisam."

In another bundle were envelolpes sent from Brooklyn, hand addressed by her father. They contained other letters addressed to her but which she had never seen. A momentary thought: Had her father intercepted messages to her from Dr. Allen of Philadelphia, whom she met thirty years earlier while painting Grace and Edith Howe at their home on Locust Street? Had he willfully thwarted the youthful relationship between his daughter and the doctor? If so, for what reason, and why would he have sent them to Lizzie? Had he sought her support in keeping Dr. Allen and Louise apart? Louise was fearful of knowing. She threw the bundle into the wastebasket beside the desk.

Questions persisted and, hands trembling, she retrieved one letter from the bundle to find the words of her Philadelphia beau that had been written in ink were by now faded, blurred and unreadable. She had long forgotten their last meeting — the carriage accident in Fairmount Park and the trifling injury it caused — until she read the letter. Though she had been only slightly bruised, the bump on her nose would cause concern for the rest of her life. The Allen letters, deteriorated with age, never revealed his true feelings.

Opening another pack of letters, Louise discovered a wedding invitation. Cream-colored and formal, it revealed another period of her life, one about which she often had longed to ask Wisam. Louise smiled, then tears began to flow, and finally she sank to the floor with convulsive sobs.

CHAPTER

2

'BEREFT OF WIFE & CHILD'

Mr. John Dyer
requests the pleasure of your company
at the Marriage Reception of his daughter,
Grace Eugenia Dyer,
to J. B. Francis Herreshoff
on Wednesday, February ninth, 1876
from half past four to half past six o'clock,
11 Charles Field St., Providence, R.I.

The Dyer family in February 1876 had depended upon Lizzie to make the major arrangements for her sister Grace's wedding. Lizzie's ability to perform this duty aside, she would never have permitted another to take on the responsibility. Though not the eldest sister, she was the most able. Two older sisters, Frances and Louisa, married with children, lived in Boston. Of the younger, Lucy had been chronically ill for most of her life and Cornelia seemed born to follow Lizzie's instructions.

The wedding and reception proved Lizzie's mettle. The gas jets were opened wide at 11 Charles Field Street, and the heavily polished brass chandeliers were set aglow. The intricately carved roses, ivy leaves, clusters of grapes with darting chameleons winding in every direction on the fixture's branches, added to their gleaming beauty throughout the reception rooms, the center hall, parlor, dining room and library. Etched glass globes reflected diverse patterns on the walls. John Dyer and his daughters received more than a hundred guests against a backdrop of polished walnut and mahogany furniture with attached garlands of wooden fruit and nuts intricately carved by German craftsmen; carpets from the Far East; oil paintings of ancestors in heavy gold-leaf frames; prints and steel engravings; "Old Paris" chinaware from France, with a magenta-and-gold border on the stark white surface; coffee and tea kettles with serving pieces of sterling and silver plate; and greenery and out-of-season flowers ordered from Boston. Carriage after carriage arrived at the covered stoop supported by classical Ionic columns.

The Dyer daughters were dressed in the latest styles from patterns in *Godey's Lady's Book,* and the bride-to-be was "angelic," as one guest described her, and "a porcelain figurine," according to another, in ivory satin and taffeta with Belgian point lace.

The walnut-wood wedding table, normally round, was extended with six matching leaves. White candles in silver sticks of telescopic design, and the cloth of delicate linen damask on which they sat, drew many compliments. The centerpiece was a three-tiered porcelain Old Paris stand with covered pots de crème from the hundred-piece service that the late Mrs. Dyer had purchased in Boston from the Alfred Douglas Company. The fragile covered cups were intertwined with fresh, green ivy and clusters of small grapes, flanked by standing tazzas of nut meats, trays of turkey and ham, venison, compotes of various salads and Miss Waterman's 32½ pounds of wedding cake with candied fruits and delicate spices. Coffee poured into demitasses and tea from the Orient served in Chinese porcelain cups were placed on the sideboard. Spirits and wines from Portugal and France in crystal carafes rested

A FRAGILE UNION

THE DYER HOME, 11 CHARLES FIELD STREET,
IN PROVIDENCE, 1876

on the marble-top table in the center of the library.

With marriage vows exchanged, the radiantly happy couple joined the guests for the social reception that followed. The melodies of a five-piece orchestra flowed from the center hall throughout the home.

Changing into traveling clothes shortly before six, Gracie and Frank, serenaded by the musicians, left on their honeymoon trip to Washington, the nation's capital, a city aglow and decorated in its finest manner celebrating the centennial of Independence. A suite, reserved far in advance, awaited the young couple at the grand Willard Hotel.

In Providence, the Dyer family congratulated themselves until nearly midnight on how well the party had gone and how well the Dyers had lived up to the social standards undoubtedly expected by the Herreshoffs. After all, Grace had married into one of New England's grandest families.

Following tradition, Lizzie, Lucy and Cornelia placed pieces of the cake under their pillows, each fervently hoping that the next wedding would be hers. The spiced cake's miraculous powers failed to meet their promise; the three sisters, all senior to Grace, remained unmarried for the rest of their lives.

Soon after arriving in Washington, a letter reached Grace in the honeymooners' suite at the Willard.

Feb. 11, 1876
Providence

My dear Grace,

I suppose by this time you may realize that you are really married but it seems very strange to us and I fear it will be some time before we come to the full realization of the fact. To think that little Gracie has been and gone to be married. The wedding certainly was a great success. The bride received a great many compliments and I think you may feel perfectly satisfied. I hope you did not get so tired that you could not rest.

Louise's mother, Grace Dyer Herreshoff, 1876

Standing so long must have been very wearisome. Minnie came in this morning to see your dress, the waist more particularly. She admired the waist very much and thought it looked as though it was made onto you. She never saw anything fitted more beautifully.

Mrs. Herreshoff, Sallie and Julian were in this morning. They said Mrs. Wards and Mrs. Abbott thought you were dressed beautifully and that everything passed off as nicely as possible. Mrs. Abbott has always taken a great fancy to you, and thought your train was beautiful. Mrs. Wards invited the Herreshoffs to stay over night there. Dr. Wood was there and remembered Grandpa Chamberlain and talked over our family in Boston. Mrs. Robinson was very loud in her praises; she always admired you very much, thought your neck looked like marble, so Clara Henderson said she could not keep her eyes off you. I don't think there is any harm in telling you these things. You can bear them.

We all think Frank looked his best and on the whole I may add a very fine looking couple. Dr. Mathis thought it as pleasant a wedding as he ever attended, thought the table very beautiful and others speak of it, so I see nothing to regret. You went off in such a hurry I am afraid you did not have your things just as I should have liked them. If you want your lace handkerchief I will send it to you.

When we were eating some of the goodies this morning, I was just about to ask where Gracie was, then I thought. The rooms are about restored to their former condition.

We all liked the music very much. Did you notice how joyfully the band played you off and just as soon as the carriage drove off they wound up. Everyone thinks Dr. Taylor performed the ceremony very satisfactory. We are all very much pleased with his words. Mr. Stockbridge said Dr. Taylor almost dreaded to do it. I think he tried to do his very best and succeeded. We all send you and Frank a great deal of love. We shall expect to hear by tomorrow something from you.

I need hardly say to tell Frank to take the very best of care of you. I know he will but we can hardly feel to give you up as yet but we shall get used to the idea in time and after all you are the same Gracie.

Love affectionately,
Sister Lizzie

Following their honeymoon, Brooklyn became the couple's new home as they took up residence at a fashionable boarding house at 62 South 9th Street in the Williamsburgh neighborhood, north of elegant Brooklyn Heights. They quickly settled into married life, Grace as an earnest young wife attempting to master the traditional duties of managing at home and Frank as a scientist with the Nichols Chemical Company on Long Island. As Frank's scientific and professional achievements continued, he was promoted, first to manager, then to superintendent at one of the nation's largest chemical concerns.

In 1876, Frank became a founding member of the American Chemical Society. Social recognition and financial stability followed. Mr. and Mrs. William H. Nichols of the chemical firm along with members of Frank's family living in New York introduced the young couple into their circles of friends. Frank was asked to join Brooklyn's prestigious Hamilton Club, a social and professional honor sought by many but attained by relatively few.

To the family's great joy, Grace announced in early April that she was expecting; the baby was due in November. Frank, jubilant with the news, began looking for a grander home in Brooklyn, one that signified both his delight at prospective fatherhood and his growing professional success. Six months later, the expectant parents moved into 134 Montague Street in Brooklyn Heights.

In November, at Frank's request, Lizzie came from Providence to be with her sister during the remaining weeks of her pregnancy. Lizzie was a comfort to Grace and quickly assumed the role of mistress of the house, with the help of a maidservant from Hendrickson Select Agency. Frank was grateful for Lizzie's efficient, caring assistance.

By early winter, Grace, physically small and delicate, had come to term but not without several intermittent spasms as she reached the last days of her confinement. It was obvious that the much-anticipated birth would be difficult. On November 28, 1876, Dr. William Gilfillan was summoned by Mrs. Agnew, the nurse. The prolonged parturition began. By the second day of labor, no one believed that Grace or the unborn child would survive.

Both did.

On the evening of November 29, with Grace exhausted and deep in a coma-vigil, Louise Chamberlain Herreshoff, petite and beautiful, was placed in Lizzie's loving arms. A bond formed which would occasionally bend but never break. The relationship between Louise and Wisam would endure until Lizzie's casket was closed and the John Dyer vault at Mount Auburn Cemetery was covered with earth forever.

◆

Lizzie, torn by the demands of caring for a still-weak Grace and the need to return to Providence to attend her ailing sister Lucy, left Brooklyn reluctantly in mid-December for Providence and the Dyer home on Charles Field Street.

Slowly, Grace began to regain some of her strength, although she never fully recovered. Baby Louise was cared for by Mrs. Agnew, who had assisted Dr. Gilfillan at the birth. Grace, the nurse and infant Louise took short shopping walks to purchase Christmas presents to be sent to Providence. Louise, bundled in a goose down comforter, was barely visible in the folding perambulator, which had been invented, coincidentally, by her uncle James Herreshoff.

Thank-you letters arrived from Providence:

Providence
December 28, 1876

My Dear Gracie,
   You can imagine exactly how it was. After breakfast as soon as the rooms were righted we all came up to the front room and opened the box. It was the only box so all our interest was concentrated on that particular one. I shall only speak for myself, as the others are to reply for themselves. I was very much pleased with my gift, as it was exactly what I most wanted. I think the gloves are very handsome and think you were very kind to get them. I shall enjoy wearing them exceedingly. The pattern is very pretty indeed and I am sure no one would imagine they were anything but the solid article. I think everything you sent is as nice as could be desired.
   Father is very much pleased with his handkerchiefs. I wish one could have done more for you but you know how we are situated. The handkerchiefs are as fine, finer than one could wish. I think you did splendidly in all your purchases. It must have taken some money.
   About noontime Father came home with a box from Louisa. You may draw on your imagination a second time. As it was directed to Father, he cut the cords for a second time. She duplicated your present to Father, one dozen handkerchiefs, but he will need them all in time. I may say here without any detriment to Louisa, only for your satisfaction, yours are a little larger and finer. Then as she did not know what to send us, she sent us all a $2 piece, and the children sent some Christmas cards.
   We gave Ellen, the maid, a calico dress and a ruffled apron and gave Father a clothes brush. I wish the Nichols had invited you; it made us feel kind of homesick for you when you wrote in regard to Christmas. How I wish we could all be together. How cunning is the dear baby? I see a good many silk cloaks. If Frank gives you the money I would get it if I could afford it. No more news.

With much love,
Lizzie

From John Dyer:

My Daughter,
I thank you most kindly for remembering me among the number you have given to, the handkerchiefs you selected for me were just what I wanted, and such nice ones too, I appreciate them. I hope you have had a Merry Christmas, a kiss for the baby and two for yourself.
My regards to Francis.

Your Father

Lizzie returned to Brooklyn after the Christmas season to care for Grace and Louise. Frank wanted Louise to know her grandfather and aunts, so he encouraged Lizzie to take Louise along on her infrequent trips back to Providence. Doting family attention, quite different from any she received at home in Brooklyn, made the trips exciting for little Louise.

Grace became pregnant for the second time in March 1880. On December 2, she began her sixth day of labor. Five hours into it, she suffered an embolism of the heart. Mother and unborn child died. Over the next few months, Lizzie shielded Louise from the sorrow by distraction and removal from the home where gloom prevailed. At the same time, Lizzie attempted to console Frank in his depth of grief.

Little Louise remained in Bristol with her father's family during the funeral services for her mother in Providence and the burial in the Dyer family vault at Mount Auburn. The day after the entombment, Frank, Lizzie and Louise returned to Brooklyn. Lizzie's position in the Herreshoff household was now firmly established. She enthusiastically embraced her new role as helpmate to Frank and surrogate mother to three-year-old Louise.

Frank admired Lizzie for the love and support she brought to the family during the four years of his marriage to Grace. But admiration was the extent of his feeling toward her. For Lizzie, unfortunately, the opposite was the case. From Providence, John Dyer and Lizzie's sisters encouraged — and expected — a union between Lizzie and Frank after an acceptable period of mourning.

Six months after Grace's death, John Dyer wrote his daughter:

Providence, May 25, 1881

My Dear Lizzie,
    Your letter is at hand and we have considered of what you thought of saying to Frank. We think it would be just the right thing. Lucy says you should certainly have the talk with Frank about marriage and use the exact language that you wrote us and you should impress upon him that it is a great pleasure to do for him as well as Louise. I should tell him that you are willing to do all you can to make it pleasant for him. Lucy says she hopes you will say what you propose about always having the care of Louise.
    Lucy is not as well today as she expected. The pains came on again last evening. She feels brighter this afternoon.
    Give my regards to Frank and love to Louise and many kisses and tell Frank the next time he comes to Bristol be sure and come here, as I am always glad to see him.

From Father

Lizzie's talk with Frank, better described as a tearful proposal, did not produce the results she so longed for. The tone of her voice and her words vacillated between sweetness and bitterness. Frank, nine years younger than Lizzie, was disinclined to marry her, deeply though her family desired it. Even so, the Dyers urged Lizzie to remain in Brooklyn to be with Louise, as her maternal attachment was as close as that of mother and child.

Feigning illness, John Dyer wrote Lizzie in the spring of 1881, requesting that she come to Providence. Frank allowed Louise, now four, to accompany her aunt. He never suspected that John Dyer's "illness" would become protracted and be

followed by an exacerbation of sister Lucy's chronic bron-
chial condition.

John Dyer's and Lucy's health was not the only reason
Lizzie would concoct to delay returning to Brooklyn. Three
months later, she wrote to Frank: "Louise has a slight fever
from a cold. We are invited to a wedding in Roxbury and Louise would love to go."

Louise's visit to Providence with Lizzie stretched from
May 1881 to the following January, despite Frank's wishes that
his daughter be home by autumn. Though his life was increasingly dominated by his career, he nonetheless longed to have
Louise home again:

Brooklyn, January '82

Dear Lizzie,
    I was glad to get your letter the other day and to learn
again that your father still continues to improve. I shall hope
to hear soon that he is sitting up. You will give him my best
wishes and congratulate him on his great courage and reserve
strength.
    The last cold wave it went down to 3 below zero here.
It froze in the kitchen but I kept the water running and the
pipes did not freeze. If I get too cold I can soon warm up with
the pulley weights.
    I am glad to hear that little Louise is well and happy and
full of life. She must indeed be a great comfort to you all. I miss
her very much and hard as it seems I know that she is safe in
your hands. When I compare her with strangers and all that is
wicked in this world, I may well feel proud that she is surrounded with love and tenderness, my heart beats with joy for her. It
seems the only recompense for the loss of her dear mother.
    I am very busy at the works and some improvements of
late that have turned out entirely satisfactory have afforded
me great pleasure. I have been twice to Harry Earles to play
billiards. Mr. & Mrs. C.H. Nichols have invited me to a musical
party at their house. I must close with a kiss for Louise.

Affectionately yours,
J. B. Francis Herreshoff

The delay in returning Louise to her father continued for another two months. Then, nearly sixteen months after Grace's death, Frank wrote a letter to Lizzie with news that would be received with the force of a violent Nor'easter, shaking the very foundation of the house and the Dyer family on Charles Field Street.

Brooklyn, March 28, 1882

Dear Lizzie,

I was glad to get your letter the other day and to learn your father still improves. I was sorry that dear little Louise had been sick, and it's pleasant to know that she soon got well again. She must look very cunning on her roller skates. I hope she had good luck having her pictures taken. I have also had some taken and will send one on as soon as they are done. I send you a check with this.

I have been intending to tell you before this that of late I have been quite attentive to a young lady, a cousin of the Earles whom I met in February. Miss Emilie Duval Lee of Philadelphia and for the last three Sundays I have visited her in Philadelphia and our mutual admirations have finally resulted in our engagement of marriage. Miss Lee is a very lovely young lady of great refinement, and always joyous, kind and happy in her ways. Her mother, a charming lady, was one of the Lothrops of whom you may know. Her father was a noted physician and died a year ago. She has an older married sister and two brothers. They move in Philadelphia's best and oldest society. She is a member of the Episcopal Church. She is about as tall as you or nearly so and about the same weight — is of blond type — blue-gray eyes, very long eye lashes and light brown hair — regular and not large features. As classes among beauties, she would be described as more refined and lovely appearing, than simply extremely pretty or grandly beautiful. She is nineteen years old.

Please confine the news to your family until the end of this week when our friends may know it. This act of mine may seem strange but I know it is for the best. It will not and cannot take away any of the memories of our dear Grace. The binding, linking dear little Louise will ever tend to keep up the great admiration, kindly feeling and love I have always held for you all.

I am very busy at the works but remain in my usual good health. I hope Louise goes out of doors as much as possible. I long to see her again. Sending a kiss to her, I remain affectionately yours,

J. B. Francis Herreshoff

Frank enclosed a picture of his fiancée. Lizzie ripped it to pieces and never showed Louise.

If the various maladies of John Dyer, Lucy or little Louise described by Lizzie in letters to Frank were exaggerated or invented, surely the news contained in Frank's letter was enough to cause all the Dyers to become ill. The first thoughts and questions were of Louise and how the relationship with Lizzie would be changed by the entry of Miss Lee into the family. Frank's letter was dissected word by word until each Dyer knew it by heart. Each sentence prompted an angry question. How could he remarry so soon after the death of dear Grace? How, as a distinguished man of thirty-two, could he marry a girl hardly more than half his age? How dare he compare this Philadelphia belle's physical characteristics with Lizzie's? As Frank's success with Nichols Chemical grew, so did his financial support of the Dyers; would they continue to receive his largess?

The answers were not immediately forthcoming, and to some questions no answers existed. Julia Herreshoff, Frank's mother, may have eased some of the concerns or she may have raised others when she wrote the Dyers three days later.

Bristol, R. I. March 31st, 1882
To the Father and Sisters of my dear Grace:

My very dear friends,
Francis announced to us his engagement to Miss Lee and that he would write your family the next day. So you must have heard on this date. It is needless to say how many tender recollections this news must awaken in your minds, as it does in my own, and among all our family, for we were very much

attached to Grace. Since Lucy's last attack there seemed very little prospect that Lizzie could take Francis' darling to him at least until autumn. I urged him marrying again if he found one that could fill Grace's place, all that she would have been had she been spared to him. I also wrote that since Mr. Dyer had so far recovered it was very likely Lizzie would take his child to him next autumn and keep house for him another winter but should it be otherwise I sincerely hoped he might find another companion who would be to him what our dear Gracie would have been had she lived. Think of Francis bereft of wife and child. I think it more probable that some years would have elapsed before another matrimonial connection, had circumstances allowed Lizzie to remain at his house with his dear and only child.

I long to see my dear little granddaughter and when the weather is suitable if either of you can be spared, I hope you will come down and pass a day at least. You know we all shall be pleased to have you stay longer but perhaps you would rather come when the weather is more settled. Many congratulations on your recovery Mr. Dyer and with love from Mr. Herreshoff and myself to you all.

Sincerely,
Julia A. Herreshoff
(Mrs. Charles F. Herreshoff)

Julia Herreshoff's letter did little to appease the Dyers. On the contrary: It increased their anger and resentment. Any suggestion that Lizzie should return to Brooklyn as maidservant to Frank, for whom her love had been completely unrequited, and to his new bride twenty-two years her junior, was more than Lizzie could bear.

Seething with anger, jealousy and hurt, Lizzie wrote to Frank. His response made clear the contents of her letter:

Brooklyn, April 6th '82

Dear Lizzie,

Your letter of the 30th was duly received, it was by no means such a letter as I had expected to receive from you and probably took me more by surprise than the news of my letter to you. Only those of morbid puritanical ideas of this life could be shocked by what I have done. Those who look upon life in an everyday practical manner will certainly agree with me. You would have me remain in gloom and solitude for years, or better, never remarry at all, while I take the greatest pride in showing the world that I am man enough to brave any misfortune however great.

Our dear Grace's death is also a very fresh event for me, and always will be as long as I live. Her loss is a great one, but fortunately it's a wise provision in the marriage act that this great loss can be restored. I do not expect to be married at present; neither do I expect to wait two years. I never knew before that two years is the shortest allowable time in such cases. Of course, everyone does not think alike about this, but many of my friends who know me well express their great approval of what I have done. They do not consider it an injustice to myself but a sound move. I am sorry I have done anything to displease you, but I am sure I cannot please everyone.

I am surprised that you place so much importance on the part of Gracie's dying message, withheld from me, for such a statement could only come from her with her mind in a state of delirium and not in her right mind. What true woman loving her husband as Grace did, what loving mother, loving her child as she did, and knowing the love of that father for his daughter could wish after her death that dear little child should be taken away from him and made to live away from his influence forever? Has a father no love for his child? Does he take no pride in bringing up to womanhood the offspring of his flesh and blood, all that he has left of that dear woman whose memory will be with him forever?

No, my heart may be kind but I cannot grant your request. I cannot give up dear little Louise; she will live in her father's house under his influence. But it shall ever be my pleasure to allow her long visits to her aunts and grandfather, whose kindness and loving treatment to her I can never forget.

I mail with this my photograph and an Easter card for dear little Louise. I hope she is well and happy. I shall hope to hear of your father's improvement and that Lucy is mending.

I am affectionately yours,
J.B. Francis Herreshoff

Frank's letter further infuriated Lizzie, and she became more determined to have Louise as her own. Did Grace in her dying moments whisper to Lizzie a wish about Louise — or had Lizzie simply imagined it as little Louise began to slip from her arms? In either case, Lizzie needed an ally, and she looked to Lewis Herreshoff, Frank's blind, unmarried brother in Bristol. Sympathetic, he visited Lizzie in Providence. Lizzie read to Lewis his mother's letter urging Frank to remarry after learning of his feelings for Emilie. Lewis disagreed with his mother's sentiments, and upon returning to Bristol, made his feelings known.

His mother wrote Lizzie:

April 1882

My dear Elizabeth,
    Lewis was so much excited yesterday afternoon on his return from Providence respecting the letter I wrote you lately, that our family would not be satisfied until they see the letter. So will you send it to me by return of mail and you shall have it again at once. With kind regards to each one of you and my love and a kiss to my granddaughter.

I remain, yours truly,
Julia A. Herreshoff

Lizzie returned Julia's letter and enclosed a letter of her own. It must have contained much of the language she had used in writing to Frank when she disclosed Grace's death-bed words. If said in her dying momtnts, the wish had been heard only by Lizzie. Did Lizzie write to Frank that she would die if Louise were taken from her? Was Grace's wish real, or imagined? Only Lizzie would ever know.

Julia shared her letter and Lizzie's with Charles, her husband, and with Frank's eight brothers and sisters. There is no question as to the internal opinions expressed. Frank and his mother had made their positions known. The other members, at least during the summer months, would form a consensus. Strong-willed Julia wrote Lizzie:

Bristol, R.I. June 14th, 1882

My dear Lizzie,
At this very late date I am writing you and enclosing my letter to you of March 31st. My delay in returning the letter to you seems almost unpardonable, it being more than two months since you wrote me. I have both letters open before me, yours and mine, after reading them over I cannot find that I committed any fault in writing as I did. You will observe where I have penciled marked and, ... my dear young friend ... how could you understand it otherwise that I meant and expressed? Circumstances did not allow of your remaining in Brooklyn while your father was so very ill in Providence, and afterwards, when he was only convalescent and Lucy taken down, would anyone in their senses think you could leave her. It seems to me that my advice to Francis was what most mothers would have given, placed as he was at the time. More than a year had passed since the death of his wife and he was receiving advice to break up his establishment, it seemed proper that his mother should express her opinion, and that he should listen to her more even than to his own sister, Sally, or any other person. And I feel quite sure that had Frank been your own brother and Grace my daughter, that your advice would have been the same as mine.
Do remember me most kindly to your father and your sisters, and a kiss for my dear little Louise and consider me most faithfully yours.

Julia A. Herreshoff

The lines were drawn. Julia Herreshoff, determined mother of nine, concerned for her son's welfare ... Lizzie Dyer, spinster, strong-willed, self-appointed protector of her niece ... Frank Herreshoff, sad and lonesome for the companionship of a wife and daughter.
And little Louise, pawn.

The struggle continued from April until August of 1882. There were numerous private family gatherings between the Dyers and the Herreshoffs. Volleys of letters, both courteous and irate, were exchanged, conversations were told and retold, and support from friends and clergy was courted vigorously. The Herreshoffs were hot-blooded and divided, the Dyers ice cold and united.

The heartrending decision came in late summer, 1882:

Brooklyn, August 25, 1882

Dear Lizzie,

It seems to be the opinion of all the Herreshoffs and many others that were Louise taken away from you it would kill you. Now if you think this would be the result she shall remain with you. I had always pictured Louise growing up happily with me. She seems the very image of her dear mother and I am sure would have afforded me great comfort and pleasure. It seems very trying to lose dear Grace and I assure you it's also trying to give up Louise but it seems that it's done to save a life, the comforter of your father and sisters in Providence, and to cheer and give pleasure to them. Without you, life with them would hardly go on, and without Louise it seems you cannot exist.

Louise has always been the pride of my life, but only the remembrances of your past kindness as well as that of your father and sisters to me, and the knowledge that Louise goes to all as a comforting angel, to give strength and happiness to those I shall ever greatly respect; it is with these feelings only that I am compelled to give her up, after long consideration.

A father's love for his child on the one hand, and a desire to reward those whose kindness he can never forget on the other hand.

In bringing up Louise I trust you will not forget to teach her to love, honor and respect her new Mama who is in more senses than one to take the place of her dear mother, Grace; for in all her ways she strongly reminds me as well as all the Herreshoffs and many others of our dear Grace. It would indeed be a terrible thing for Louise to grow up with the feeling that her new Mama is a kind of intruder in sheep's clothing.

It remains entirely with you to bring up Louise in such a way that she will love not only her father but also her new Mama, for she cannot love one and hate the other. If in future she is shown to turn a cold shoulder on those she should love it will be positive proof that you have neglected to do an important duty toward her and her father.

With a kiss for Louise and affectionately yours,

J. B. F. Herreshoff

Lizzie was victorious in the struggle. Apparently, a threat of suicide had brought Frank to the most painful decision of his life.

Lizzie honored every wish and mandate expressed in Frank's letter. Over the years a warm bond developed between Louise and Emilie Lee Herreshoff, her new stepmother, and in time with her two half-brothers, Frederick and Francis, and her half-sister Sarah.

Louise was part of two families. Lizzie, as a surrogate mother, had her precious child to raise, direct, encourage and love over the principal part of the next forty-five years.

CHAPTER

3

FAMILY REUNION

By 1882 Providence and New York had become homes to Louise, now five. Though poles apart in their influence, each city and each family would have significant but very different roles in her formative years.

Louise met her father's new wife for the first time in Bristol at the fiftieth wedding-anniversary celebration of her grandparents, Julia and Charles Herreshoff. It was Louise's first separation from Aunt Lizzie and her first meeting with "Mama Emilie." Emilie made every effort to ease the awkwardness for her stepdaughter as she, too, found the Herreshoff gathering a test of acceptance. Brother James and his Irish wife, Jane, had been the only Herreshoff family members present at her marriage to Frank. Although the majority of his family had urged his second marriage, Emilie always felt like an outsider — as did most who married into the Herreshoff family in the nineteenth century.

Aunt Lizzie had seen to it to that Louise was at her very best in manner and appearance as she left for Bristol with Ellen, the Dyers' maidservant. Her dark golden hair, with natural waves and curls, shone brilliantly in the sunlight as the family reunion portrait was taken on the steps of a Bristol inn. She wore a striped silk skirt of pale blue and ivory, a waist blouse of deeper blue with a wide ivory-colored embroidered collar.

Her stockings matched her blouse and four small buttons fastened her high-top soft, black leather shoes. She was "turned out," as some would say, but her expression betrayed the sadness of being separated from Aunt Lizzie.

As the celebration continued throughout the day, Louise met her cousin James. Slightly younger, he had been born in London, where his father, James Sr., represented the Herreshoff Manufacturing Company. Young James and Louise shared an interest in the pianoforte in the Herreshoff's living room. They sat, squeezed closely together, on the oval stool and tapped at the ivory keys. The youthful friendship continued over the years, and James and Louise would grow closer as time passed.

The celebration lasted until late afternoon, when Louise returned to Providence and to Aunt Lizzie. Louise answered few, if any, of the many questions the Dyers eagerly asked. They were unaware that young cousin James would be Louise's only happy memory of the day.

Louise's religious and academic training in Providence reflected the strict moral and social standards of the Dyer family. Daily home devotionals at breakfast and supper were a Dyer ritual. Seldom did the routine change. John Dyer read aloud from the New Testament at seven each morning and his daughters took turns reading Psalms after the dining table was righted at night. For Louise, they often cited a poem from the American Baptist Publication Society:

"Help for Children and the Friends of Children"

Happy the child whose early years
    Receive instruction well
Who hates the sinners past and fears
    The road that leads to hell.
When we devote our youth to God
    'Tis pleasing in his eyes,
A flower when offered in the bed
    Is no vain sacrifice.

HERRESHOFF FAMILY REUNION, 1883

'T will save us from a thousand snares
   To mind religion young
Grace will preserve our following years,
   And make our virtue strong.
Let the sweet word of prayer and praise
   Employ my youngest breath,
Thus I'm prepared for longer days,
   Or fit for early death.

Louise sat motionless, listening to the readings at home and to sermons at Sunday morning and evening services in the Dyer pew No. 56 at the First Baptist Meeting House. Her great-great uncle Joseph Brown had designed the church, an architectural triumph, in the late eighteenth century.

Her aunts' diary entries for each Sunday were summaries of the pastor's words to the congregation:

Sunday, 20 January

   Good Dr. Swain preached John 4:35,36. A very humbling sermon. Went to Sunday school, also to evening meeting. Felt very humble. Saw Dr. Swain to talk with, going in and coming out.

Sunday, 10 February

   Went to church all day. Dr. Thompson preached from Acts 2:36 and John 3:10.

Sunday, 24 February

   Dr. Thompson's text was from the American Tract Society, "Sinners welcome to come to Jesus Christ. Though your sins be as scarlet, they shall be as white as snow."

Diary entries varied little:

   Went to church this afternoon. We must all appear before the judgment seat of Christ. I then the prisoner of the Lord be.

   A very rainy morning went to church late and heard a part of Dr. Swain's sermon. Went to our own pew at the Communion service. Went also to Missionary concert.

LOUISE, AGE 6

Continued financial support from Frank Herreshoff enabled the Dyers to maintain their comfortable living standards on Charles Field Street. Lizzie received extra funds for trips to New York and summer vacations to the seaside and mountains with Louise. Lizzie managed to keep a balance of at least $2,000, a considerable sum for the day, in her personal account at the Rhode Island Hospital Trust Company. By all measures, the Dyer family was financially quite secure.

Beginning at the age of six, Louise received, thanks to her father's support, the best formal schooling available to young girls in Providence. Studio classes in art with Miss Mary Wheeler at 26 Cabot Street made for a happy and fruitful time, and she and her art studio became major influence on Louise throughout her childhood and teenage years. Miss Wheeler's guidance differed greatly from that of an elderly grandfather and his spinster daughters. Drawing and sketching came naturally to Louise. Painting and sculpture opened new and exciting vistas, and Louise received strong direction from Miss Wheeler, herself a talented and accomplished artist who constantly encouraged in her pupils an appreciation of the arts. The training provided an opportunity to make drawings from casts and paint from models. Under her teacher's watchful eye, Louise trained early in portraiture, progressing over time through a variety of techniques.

Born in Concord, Massachusetts, in 1846, Mary Wheeler came of age during a time of growing civil conflict, which profoundly influenced both her social and political attitudes and her vocation. In Concord, her family closely associated with Mary Moody Emerson, aunt of Ralph Waldo Emerson, and the Alcotts, whose daughters would join Mary Wheeler for travel and study in Europe. David Thoreau, who would pass the Wheeler house on his daily walks to Walden Woods, and Nathaniel Hawthorne were among her neighbors.

When she was eleven, Mary attended an oration in the Concord Town Hall. The speaker was John Brown, the famous abolitionist, who railed against the evils of slavery. She was deeply moved. Two years later, in December, 1859, she returned to the hall to attend a memorial service following his death at Harper's Ferry. The tribute, organized by A. C. Alcott, included eulogies from Emerson and Thoreau. F. B. Sandborn's "Dirge" would long be remembered:

> Today, beside Potomac's way
> Beneath Virginia's Sky
> They slay the man who loved the slave
> And dared for him to die

Mary began her teaching career at Miss Shaw's finishing school in Providence. Extensive travel and study in Germany, Britain and France helped her sharpen her artistic talents and exposed her to styles of painting that were just then emerging.[1]

It was Mary Wheeler who first recognized Louise's artistic talent, and she encouraged Louise to send a sketch and a drawing to her father in Brooklyn. Frank Herreshoff's acknowledgment arrived a few days later.

Brooklyn, April 11/84

My dear little Louise:
    I was delighted with the two very fine letters you sent me. Your handwriting greatly surprised and delighted me. I could hardly believe it came from my dear little Louise. Before I opened the envelope of your first letter I wondered what businessman in Providence had written to me, and you may imagine my surprise to find inside a letter from you. I showed your paintings to Mr. Nichols and he thought them so fine that he took them out to show to his children ... I hope you are

---

1 *Mary C. Wheeler, Leader in Art and Education,* by Blanche E. Wheeler Williams, 1934

strong and well and regular at your meals. You must not neglect to eat plenty of simple food and not candies. I hope you will enjoy Easter. Give my love to your grandpa and aunt and believe me,

Affectionately your father,
J.B.F. Herreshoff

Louise was seven years old when she received her father's praise of her penmanship and her art. This could well have been her first art review, but others would come.

In addition to her instruction at the Wheeler School, Louise studied mathematics, the classics, French, German and English at the Lincoln School, a few blocks away from the Dyer residence. It was an appropriate curriculum for bringing up a proper young woman in nineteenth-century New England. But it was Louise's natural talent for painting — especially portraiture — that blossomed in daily studio classes and private instruction under the watchful eye of Mary Wheeler. She was beginning — at least insofar as her formal education was concerned — to oblige her Aunt Cornelia's wish that she "give the impression of being the niece of wealthy and stylish aunts."

The heat of summer in Providence sent many of the city's families of means to fashionable mountain and seaside resorts. In keeping with the custom, Aunt Lizzie and Louise would retreat to New England coastal towns such as Gloucester and Rockport in Massachusetts and Ogunquit in Maine. Louise was seldom without her watercolor box, oils, brushes, sketchpad and canvas to record the hillside flowers and trees or the rocky beaches of New England's seacoast. During these holidays Louise and Lizzie were rarely apart.

When she was fifteen, Frank Herreshoff wrote to daughter at Shattuck Farm in Jeffrey, New Hampshire:

LOUISE CHAMBERLAIN HERRESHOFF IN 1892, AGE 16

The Hamilton Club Brooklyn, N.Y.
Aug. 29, 1892

My dear little Louise:
 If you gain every two months to come as in the two just passed, I shall have to call you big Louise. I am glad to learn you have had such a pleasant time in the country. I hope your future summers will be spent as pleasantly. I hope you can keep yourself always in good health and your mind and body always pleasantly employed. I am sure you are then likely to continue in happiness. How pleasant it must be for you to have friends and playmates with you, and also to find those near you, who like you, enjoy painting, art, and all the beauties of nature to be found in the country. Such pursuits and such occupations as you enjoy appeal to all that is high, pure and noble in your walk of life and must result in a sound and lasting benefit to you. I hope you will return to the city quite refreshed in mind and body and ready to enter into the duties of this life with a newness and earnest vigor.
 I have been up to the mountains every two weeks. Your Mama and the children are well. Francis fell into the lake and went under but came up, got hold of the boat and was pulled ashore. He was out again with a suit of dry clothes in half an hour. Minnie, the maid fell down the mountainside, cut her head and came near being killed. It's a little late and I must go to 12 Pierrepont for sleep. I send a check for $75. Much love to your Aunt Lizzie, your grandpa and all, and with much love for yourself.

Sincerely, your loving Papa
J B F Herreshoff

 Louise traveled frequently to New York with Aunt Lizzie to visit her father, stepmother Emilie and half siblings, who by then resided on Pierrepont Street in Brooklyn Heights. Emilie brought to the family the style and sophistication of a Philadelphia socialite, and she and Louise developed a close relationship. If Aunt Lizzie was jealous, she never showed it. After all, she shared greatly in the attention and financial support being lavished upon Louise, though she would never overcome her earlier dream of being the second Mrs. J. B. Francis Herreshoff.

Compared with Providence, New York provided a more cosmopolitan life, and exposure to the city's rich cultural and social offerings greatly influenced young Louise. Each visit exposed her to the latest fashions, visits to the museums and evenings at the theatre. The family dined regularly in the finest restaurants and at the exclusive Hamilton Club, about two blocks from the Herreshoff home. Conversations over tea at the Nicholses' home and at parties and meetings with other prominent families prepared Louise for the social demands her life would later require. From the sidewalk along the East River, she and Emilie would watch sailing ships arrive and depart the bustling port. From their earliest days together as stepmother and stepdaughter, they had been awed by the sight of the Brooklyn Bridge in the East River, which, when it opened in 1883 with a spectacular celebration of electric lights and fireworks, essentially merged Brooklyn and New York into a single metropolis. They were equally impressed by the Statue of Liberty in New York Harbor, France's glorious Centennial gift to the United States, dedicated ten years late, when Louise was nine, because it took that long to raise the money to build a pedestal.

The Herreshoff family's summer gatherings in Bristol gave Louise the opportunity to know her young cousins, the children of uncles James and Charles.

James invented baking powder while working for the Rumford Chemical Works near Providence and later would find new worlds and fortunes as he traveled from Bristol to England and the European continent with the growth of the Herreshoff Manufacturing Company. The company produced the finest sailing and racing yachts in America and found new markets by developing torpedo boats. Herreshoff racing yachts, designed and built by uncles John and Nathaniel, successfully defended the Americas Cup against Sir Thomas Lipton and others in five of the most noted championship yachting races. The Herreshoff yachts — Columbia, Resolute, Reliance and Enterprise — focused world attention on Bristol and gave rise to the city's unofficial nickname, "Yachting Capital of the World." The Herreshoffs' Bristol boatyard and its skilled craftsmen attracted customers with names of international notoriety: J. P. Morgan, William Randolph Hearst, the Vanderbilt family.

James' son, also called James, became Louise's favorite playmate as they grew from childhood to adolescence, unaware of — or, more accurately, unconcerned with — their family's greatness in many fields.

Drawing, sketching and painting remained Louise's strongest interests year after year. Her subjects reflected her childhood surroundings. She painted small sailboats, for example, with soft gray-white sails floating on pale blue seas in Narragansett Bay, with harbor mist seeming to be a veil of lifting fog.

Louise spent the summer of 1896 in Europe with Mary Wheeler and other students from the Wheeler studio. They concentrated on the classical concept of beauty and spent much of their time in Paris immersing themselves in all things French and frequenting the Musée du Louvre and the Palais du Luxembourg.

Louise returned to France the following summer with Miss Wheeler and spent several months at Fontenay-aux-roses, south of Paris, where she met Raphael Collin, a teacher and leader in the plein-air school of painting. Teacher and pupils worked amid the quaint villages and gardens. Louise again was enveloped with French culture and beauty. Regular sightseeing visits to Paris exposed her to great masterworks of painting, sculpture and architecture. She often spent her allowance on historical photographs and pieces of antique European porcelain.

Showing visible progress in her works of oils and watercolors, she returned to study with Collin for several summers. On at least one occasion Aunt Lizzie sailed over and joined her, and they visited Switzerland, among other places.

At home in Providence during the remaining months of each year, she continued her portraiture. As her skill became recognized, commissions began coming her way from Providence, New York, Bristol and Philadelphia. Family connections were helpful, but her ability to capture her subject's likeness with delicate brush strokes brought serious approbation of her work.

Financial support to pursue her artistic ambition continued to come from her father, who had profited greatly from royalties earned through his contributions to chemical engineering. Frank's development of an oven for roasting sulfuric acid as well as other major chemical processes brought wealth in addition to national and international recognition. He generously shared his good fortune with Louise and her surrogate family. His greatest recognition came in 1906 when he became the first recipient of the Perkin Medal, named for the English chemist Sir William Perkin, who discovered and developed coal-tar products. Frank was declared the most distinguished American representative of chemical discoverers and inventors. In accepting the award, he stated, "You must love chemistry better than your own soul."

Aunt Lizzie, sharing in the very liberal allowance sent by Frank to Providence would, nevertheless, feign personal needs from time to time with her Dyer relatives in Boston, thereby assuring income from there as well as from New York. Her requests for new spectacles, medicines and other professional attention would not go unfulfilled by loving but dismayed family members. It was always Frank, however, who kept the

Charles Field Street home financially secure and made possible Louise's ambition to study art.

Louise concentrated on painting portraits, using family members and close friends in both Providence and New York as models. Most were unabashedly willing to pose, and some even vied to be next in line. Immensely proud of his daughter's blooming talent, Frank for a brief period rented a studio for her in Brooklyn.

In 1897, at the age of 20, Louise made her formal debut. For the occasion, no expense was spared, and Frank saw to it that his daughter was presented to New York society in the finest vogue of the period. Frank's gift to Louise was a lovely ring with a row of five large opals.

Emilie made all the arrangements, even suggesting the color for Aunt Lizzie's party dress. Louise wrote Lizzie: "I will be wearing white, Mama will be in pink and thinks you would be lovely in gray." Lizzie thought otherwise and stood regal and rigid in a pale shade of violet in the family receiving line.

The following March, Louise wrote to Aunt Lizzie from Brooklyn:

> I arrived in Brooklyn all right and Miss Harris [the family governess] met me at the station. Mama had been out all morning and was too tired to come to the train. Last night we went to the Hamilton Club for dinner and Papa took me to the horse show. Mama had lined a lovely evening wrap for me, light green lined with white and pink striped silk and with white fur.
>
> Sunday I went to the Metropolitan Museum and fooled about there all the afternoon, and on Thursday morning I am going to the lively National Academy to see the pictures.

Little did Louise suspect that one of her own paintings, *An Interior* (plate 5), would be selected by the National Academy for its exhibition just two years later.

The letter continued:

> I am having a terrible time painting Sarah [her half sister] for she poses little and so badly. But I believe they think it looks like her so far.
>
> I expect to go to Philadelphia sometime soon and will have my eyes checked just before. Mama said you must come on to Brooklyn for my coming-out and also I could have Lucy Aldrich to receive with me.

The portrait of Sarah was never completed (plate 1).

From 1622 Locust Street, the Philadelphia home of Dr. Herbert Marshall Howe, who had commissioned Louise to paint his daughters, Edith and Grace, Louise wrote Lizzie:

> This afternoon a very nice young man is going to pose for me. He posed for me yesterday. He is very good looking, and is a cousin of the Howes . . . I have seen quite a little of him. He is sorry I'm not going to be here a little longer so he could take me about and show me things and I am sorry too. He played to me on the violin last night and we talked a steady stream all the rest of the evening. Dr. Allen, an oculist, the young man I have been talking about, was here to dinner tonight, and Grace said he was in the dumps because I would be leaving tomorrow or the next. I don't want to go to Brooklyn a bit and should prefer going about with this young man. He expects to go to Paris to study eyes and nervous diseases. He thinks it strange that my oculist didn't examine my eyes with an instrument he showed me.

Another letter described a fateful carriage ride with the young Dr. Allen:

> We came near having a terrible accident and was frightened for my life, when one of the horses of another carriage lost its head and the whole thing, horses and all, came cracking up against our coupe and hit my nose. We jumped out the other side as quickly as possible. The shaft of the other carriage ran into the lantern on my side and smashed it to bits, if it had hit a little further back it would have run straight through me.

Dr. Allen visited Louise at the Howes' home the night of the accident, and she presented the sketch of him she had finished. All agreed it was a perfect likeness, and he promised to have it framed. He and Edith Howe saw her off at the train station the next morning.

To Lizzie she wrote: "Dr. Allen is awfully nice and I am sorry to go away just as I get to know him." The goodbye at the station was the last meeting with the young man she had come to know and to like so much. To her knowledge he never visited Brooklyn, Providence or Paris. The youthful and romantic encounter was slow in fading as she refused to accept the finality of hope as time passed from day, to weeks, to more than a year.

Louise was at first unsuccessful in convincing her father that she should return to France to resume her lessons with Raphael Collin. Her stepmother sided with Louise, and the disagreement was the source of heated exchanges between Frank and Emilie. Dr. Howe of Philadelphia, recognizing Louise's talent as an artist, also encouraged Frank to allow her to continue studying with Collin. It had been at his home in Philadelphia that Louise captured on canvas his beautiful daughters, Grace and Edith, and he was heard to exclaim to the artist, "I'd give ten thousand dollars if one of my daughters could paint like you."

Bowing at last to pressure from Louise, Aunt Lizzie and Emilie, Frank eventually agreed to his daughter's return to France. Fearing that Louise would contract measles from her stepsister Sarah, Frank rented her an apartment at the nearby St. George's Hotel until her departure for France. Louise wrote Aunt Lizzie:

June 10, 1898

Dear Wisam,

    Here I am at the St. George's Hotel in a nice little apartment. Sarah has the measles and Mama thought, as I did, that it was running a great risk and that I might give it to Miss Wheeler's girls. Miss Greene, one of the girls seems very nice the more you see of her and we talked Paris most of the day.

It has been a perfect afternoon and Mama and I had a beautiful drive in the park and then to Maillards for brioches and ice cream. We then went home to 12 Pierrepont and I waited outside in the carriage while Mama went in and brought Sarah to the front steps that I might wave a goodbye to her. Mama has had the stateroom fixed with flowers I believe.

Take very good care of yourself Wisam and don't sit up in drafts and catch cold. Give my love to all, Bridget [the dog] included, and keep lots and lots for yourself. We sail tomorrow.

Louise

CHAPTER

THE PARIS SALON

Although Louise was traveling independently, her departure for Europe in June 1898 coincided with Mary Wheeler's annual trip with her art students. They set sail together from New York on the pacqueboat *La Touraine*. The happiness and carefree spirit of a young woman headed for Europe for the first time on her own was evidenced in daily letters to Lizzie.

Dear Wisam,

We are really started at last and I am settled enough to write a letter. First I want to thank you and Aunt Lucy and Aunt Connie for the beautiful flowers you sent me. They have come as fresh as possible and the stateroom is fairly filled with your flowers and Mama's. Your white roses are lovely, Wisam and so are Aunt Lucy's and Aunt Connie's pinks. You were very good to send me so many. Then there are letters too and a box from you, Wisam which I have not had time to open yet but I shall very soon. Papa came for me at the St. George this morning in a carriage and we got here twenty minutes before nine.

I think I have had the most beautiful send off with all my presents and flowers and candy and a stream of letters. Mama gave me a tremendous basket of fruit and a bottle of grape juice and brandy and champagne. I wish you could see all my flowers.

Goodbye Wisam or rather au revoir, I've been talking French quite a little.

THE LATEST FROM PARIS

LOUISE (CENTER) AND MARY WHEELER (SECOND FROM LEFT),
ATOP THE ARC DE TRIOMPHE, 1895

Another letter brought additional news from the trip, mentioning two friends who traveled with her, Caroline and Miss Greene:

> It is now sometime in the afternoon of the second day out and I haven't been ill yet as it has been so smooth. I read my steamer letters and walked the deck more than ever before. Tell Aunt Connie I was perfectly delighted with the purse and especially the three Ten Franc pieces done up so neatly, all this after she gave me the blue pin. I opened your present, Wisam and was very much pleased with the hatpin with the diamond. It is a beauty and I haven't opened all of your packages yet.
>
> Miss Wheeler and Miss Greene are walking on the deck and I think I must walk too. Caroline seems ill and keeps her head covered up all the time. We keep pretty much to ourselves and don't speak to anybody. The people are mostly French in the boat and not interesting in the least. There are fat Monks with gold crosses and fat Frenchmen who talk a great deal and smoke.
>
> I'm very much afraid it's getting rougher for there are so many white caps and I found difficulty walking downstairs just now. Aren't you glad you are on solid earth?
>
> I meant to tell you we had brioches and French chocolate for petit dejeuner this morning, also French butter, which is delicious, and French bread. In fact French everything! Caroline is sitting next to me here on deck with a wet handkerchief at her forehead and never eats anything or moves all day.

Louise seemed at first to write mostly of food:

> We had quite a respectable lunch today of beefsteak, fried potatoes, bread with butter, rhubarb with Holland cheese. Caroline has had far the worst of it and she looks so ill I should think she would want to jump overboard.

Before rough seas caused Louise to "nibble crackers in [her] steamer chair and better appreciate Caroline's *mal-de-mer*," she instructed Wisam in one of her daily letters to "stay indoors and out of the heat and make ice cream and strawberry shortcake and eat a lot and grow fat."

She wrote of her chats with Miss Wheeler as they walked the deck:

> We talk over Fontenay and Paris and you don't know how much I long to see it. We plan to sketch as soon as we reach Fontenay and Miss Wheeler has already engaged her model. I long to see some poplar trees sticking up in a row. A bus (horse drawn) will meet us in Paris and take us to Fontenay. Miss G. [Greene] makes fun of the way I count the days before we land. Just think, there are only three more days if we land Saturday and four if we don't get there until Sunday and I'm afraid we shant get there until then.

In another dispatch to Lizzie, she wrote, "I wish you could see the Monks go by with their long white gowns. They make me think of the ones we saw at Lucerne," referring to Lizzie's European visit when Louise was abroad with Miss Wheeler. "There are a lot of little kids who run about and have a beautiful time and the men play that game with the round pieces of wood."

Louise in her last day aboard ship exclaimed:

> Here we are in sight of England, and near enough to see the houses and green fields. A boat has just sailed by with brown sails and there is great excitement with the coast so near. How I wish you were here to see it all, how glad you must have been to see land when you came over alone. I shall have to pack this evening and have my trunk together as we leave by a special quick train for Paris tomorrow morning at half past seven. The bus Miss Wheeler has arranged will meet us there and take us all the way to Fontenay. I am having a beautiful time and hope you are well. Give my love to Aunt Lucy and Aunt Connie and keep lots for yourself. Goodbye for now, Louise.

After disembarking at Le Havre and heading for Paris, Louise expressed her excitement, echoed by Miss Wheeler, when they saw the Eiffel Tower in the distance:

> We couldn't sit still, but Miss G. and Caroline weren't at all excited and munched strawberries all the time. The omni-

bus de famille was ready for us and we and all the trunks got in, some outside and some inside, and drove off through the streets of Paris to the Madeleine and the Place de la Concorde and along the Seine. We could see Notre Dame in the distance and I never had such fun in my life. I could not believe my eyes that I was really seeing all those things again after all I have thought about. It smelled just the same as ever and I should have known where I was by the smell with my eyes shut. Wisam, I wish you could have seen the stream of carriages going up and down the ChampsElysees between the Arc de Triomphe and the Place de la Concorde. I am so glad you have seen it all and know all about it.

We passed along the Seine, the Latin Quarter and by Napoleon's Tomb and way out to the city gate and la Route de Paris lined with neat rows of trees. We stopped first at Miss Wheeler's home in Chatillon and walked through her garden, which is as beautiful as ever and drove here to Mme. de Viguerie where I will be living. Edward is to help later with the trunks. It is a lovely house with a beautiful terrace and garden in fruit — full of roses all in blossom and some climbing up the window.

Miss Greene and I have two nice rooms right opposite each other. I'm afraid Mme put me in the best one as mine has a little dressing room attached with washstand. I am well and enjoy every minute. Have a good time on your birthday, Wisam.

With lots of love, Louise

Mme. de Viguerie's home was an approved residence for young ladies, and nearby were the home and garden of Louise's instructor Raphael Collin.

Future letters home exuded similar enthusiasm:

I have been to Mon. Collin's garden and it looks the same as ever. Everything is so green and flourishing, like Switzerland only nicer. How I wish you could take afternoon tea with me sometimes, for your copper kettle and lamp are just the thing. You knew exactly what to give me. The fete is coming to Fontenay next Sunday so it will be very gay with confetti and merry-go-rounds. I must stop now and will do better if I ever get my steamer letters answered. I believe I have sixteen in all.

I am going to begin to paint regularly Monday morning in Collin's garden. I laid in a stock of paints and got a new white palette and ordered a strap to carry all my sketching things. I have found some beautiful places to sketch, one by an old church in Chatillon with the marketplace in front. I started a sketch yesterday from my bedroom window of the houses with red tile roofs and poplar trees and white walls and green trees.

In Paris yesterday I saw a beautiful pearl pin in a shop window, and so I decided I would rather spend my money for that than anything else. It was 100 francs. Aunt Lucy gave me 50, Aunt Connie gave me 30 and Bridget [the Dyers' dog] 15, and I had a lot more besides, that I earned. It's a beauty and very cheap for the pearl's size and good quality too. It is bigger than my diamond ring. I shall wear it this afternoon to tea at Miss Wheeler's. Forgot to say, I visited the Paris Salon and had a wonderful time, Miss Wheeler showed us all around.

I shall pay Collin for three months which is quite a good deal cheaper and pay my rent for one month, for I want to get it off my mind. You have no idea how beautiful Fontenay looks this summer. The roses are all in blossom in the garden and I never saw so many.

It has been very rainy today, but I began painting in the shed. Miss Greene has not started to paint yet and doesn't seem very anxious to. I can't imagine anyone taking so little interest in things, can you?

Louise's dedication and discipline to her work and her underlying true love of art were never in question. Seldom a day passed when she was without her sketchbook or watercolors or oils. Sensitive to Collin's criticism, she became more determined not only to please her teacher but, more important, to please herself. It was this trait that caused Louise gradually to begin experimenting with new subjects and techniques. Future visits to museums and galleries with her old friends the Aldriches of Providence, Miss Wheeler, and Monsieur Collin and his wife, Blanche, in Paris and throughout Western Europe and England, provided an exposure to the "Revolution in Art" that swirled at the turn of the century.

The fruit of Louise's efforts came when her plein-air painting *Le Répos* was selected for exhibition at the 1900 Paris Salon of the Société des Artistes Français. "Can you imagine a small one like Louise painting this?" Collin asked proudly.

Thus at the young age of twenty-three Louise found her name published in the catalogue of Europe's most prestigious art exhibition. It was an accomplishment she could only have dreamed of as she prepared her canvas and palette each day to record the varied scenes and subjects she found inspiring.

Family and close friends at home in America soon learned of her achievement. Frank, bursting with pride, increased her allowance. Uncle Lewis mailed letters of congratulations with money enclosed. Louise would celebrate by buying Parisian hats and couturier dresses on the Rue St-Honoré. A large diamond ring and a strand of natural pearls from a renowned Place Vendôme jewelry salon were among her first purchases.

Louise, with new confidence and ambition, moved from Fontenay to Paris and established her own apartment and studio at 145 Boulevard Montparnasse. Without the direct paternal guidance of her father or the strong maternal force of Aunt Lizzie, Louise would have, for one short period of her life, a joyful measure of independence and self-assurance.

Except for a short platonic interlude in Philadelphia, when she met Dr. Allen, the young oculist friend of the Howe family, Louise's adult life had been dominated by strong women who surrounded her. Her aunts, Lizzie, Lucy and Cornelia, her stepmother Emilie, her teacher, Mary Wheeler, the Aldrich sisters and more recently Blanche Collin had all caused mixed and confusing emotions as she grew out of her teen years.

Louise's move from Fontenay to Paris had in part been owing to the overbearing and omnipresent Blanche Collin. Mme. Collin became most aggressive with postcards, notes and letters written to Louise throughout her years in Europe, and continuing until Louise returned to New York. Invitations

LOUISE, THE PARISIENNE, 1900

to rendezvous in Italy, Germany or southern France for short vacations went unanswered.

Aunt Cornelia, at home in Providence, could rest assured that Louise continued to "give the impression of being the niece of wealthy and stylish aunts," a wish she had expressed when Louise was only a small child.

Aunt Lizzie, though terrified of sea voyages, booked passage immediately to be with Louise. Again sailing the Atlantic, she remained most of the time in her stateroom, thinking intermittently of Louise's artistic honor and the stormy ocean swells.

With her move to Paris in 1900 and her newly independent life came a totally new direction for her art. She succeeded in being placed in the ladies' studio at the Académie Julian, the atelier founded in 1868 by Rodolphe Julian. Initially he had provided classes in which male and female students, working together, sketched and painted nude models. Julian was sharply criticized for these mixed classes, and in the 1870s he abandoned the revolutionary idea and established traditional, separate studios for men and women.

It was at "the Julian" that Louise came under the influence of the artist John Paul Laurens. Noted for his historic murals, Laurens stressed the use of brilliant colors and may well have directed Louise toward her development of brighter, stronger pigments.

Louise's passionate love of color became increasingly evident:

> I bought seven new petticoats, each a different color … the flower vendor on the corner was so happy when I asked for a bunch of lilies and roses in every color he had … don't you think a solid red rug will go beautifully with my wall paper with small yellow flowers and my furniture painted white …?

Examples of French, German and Oriental porcelains, all decorated vibrantly, often appeared in her still life paintings.

Louise experimented with miniature portraits on porcelain, and at one point during this period she painted Aunt Lizzie. The small but exact likeness clearly exhibited Louise's competence even under the limitations of reduced scale.

In the same year, Frank Herreshoff, accompanied by his nephew James Herreshoff Jr., attended the seventy-fifth Annual Exhibition at New York's National Academy of Design. Louise's father had submitted one of his daughter's oils that had recently arrived from Paris. The ethereal painting, *An Interior, Number 113 (Un Intérieur)* (plate 5) was selected by the jury for inclusion. The portrait of a young lady sewing, possibly dreaming of her love, was masterfully executed. The morning sunlight streaming through the window, falling softly on the subject's slender, delicate hands, with a gentle breeze, conceivably off Narragansett Bay, causing a slight flutter of the curtains, mentally transported James Jr. to summers in Bristol and the Herreshoff family home where they shared infrequent but memorable visits. Could it be a self-portrait? No matter, for he knew at the moment he stood before the painting that his feelings for his cousin Louise were more than those of a youthful friendship.

Ten days later a lengthy letter from James arrived at Louise's Montparnesse studio apartment. James congratulated her on her recognition by the Paris Salon and the National Academy, and told her of his own early exploits in engineering and chemistry while attending the University of California. But it was his fond recollection of their summer days sailing together on Narragansett Bay, escaping the watchful eyes of the large clan of Herreshoffs, that was the principal subject of his letter.

Louise, too, remembered their times together well. Alone, she read and reread every word. Happily, James's first letter and the many that followed encouraged the best in her art. Her father, pleased with her success at the Paris Salon and at the National Academy, was convinced that Paris was indeed the center of the art world and agreed to extend her stay abroad. Louise remained until 1903, stretching her one year to five.

Three superior teachers, each using a different technique, left a lasting mark on Louise and her work during this early, formative period. Mary C. Wheeler in America and Europe opened a world of beauty and stressed academic discipline. Louise's earliest portraits show Miss Wheeler's influence, and her adventurous experimentation is evident throughout Louise's transition.

Raphael Collin at Fontenay-aux-roses built on Louise's academic foundation and added plein-air training. Daily instruction and criticism from this distinguished exhibitor and exhibition medalist would propel her works to higher levels of recognition. *Le Répos* and *Girl in Garden* (plates 4 and 6), each selected for the Paris Salon, in 1900 and 1903 respectively, reflected Collin's influence.

Jean-Paul Laurens of the Académie Julian, a professional artist and teacher of international renown, completed the trio. Laurens was a perennial favorite of American students for his use of vivid color. "Color, pure color," he would admonish. Louise spent three years under his close tutelage, and his influence is perhaps most evident in *Female Nude,* in red chalk, and in *Vase of Roses* and *Poppies* (back cover), both in oil. In his later career, Laurens became noted both in France and abroad for his classical and military murals of great dimension. His mural depicting Washington and Cornwallis at Yorktown was painted for the Baltimore Courthouse in Maryland. At his death, France would honor Laurens with full military honors.

On short trips away from Paris and the Académie, Louise painted watercolors of vivid fields of yellow rape, reminiscent of the mustard plants in America. She captured other colorful blooms in Claude Monet's garden next door to Miss Wheeler's

A FRAGILE UNION

SANS SOUCI, FREDERICK THE GREAT'S PALACE, POTSDAM

BOYHOOD HOME OF LOUISE'S GREAT-GRANDFATHER

house in Giverny. When she painted seascapes along the coast of Normandy, she mixed sands from the coastal shore in with the oils on her palette. Experimentation with medium and subject matter kept Louise's works brilliant, alive and among the avant garde of American artists.

Unlike her whirlwind travels with Miss Wheeler in earlier years to the countries of the "Grand Tour," now she selected sites that were artistically pleasing and challenging. Daily Louise would mail postcards and letters to Wisam and James from each of her stops. Her notes and their responses differed in their expressions of love.

Travel with the Aldrich family, mostly by private coach, offered new vistas in London and along the western coast of England, into Wales and Scotland. "Here I am in London at Brown's Hotel with the Aldrich family," she wrote Aunt Lizzie. "Lucy has her own apartment. High tea in the paneled lounge is sufficient for the day, but we will join again for dinner around eight. My clothes hardly fit." She added, "Lucy's father thinks Papa is very wealthy."

From 1901 to 1903, while studying at the Julian, she traveled throughout western Europe. Writing Aunt Lizzie from Pompeii, she noted: "Here I am on top of Mt. Vesuvius in a pouring rain. We went to the edge of the crater and looked in and were nearly choked by the smoke. Stuart, the guide, and I came up together. I hope we will get down alive. It seems rather doubtful. With much love, Louise"

From Italy she headed east, first to Switzerland then to Prague, with stops in Meissen, Dresden and Potsdam (the childhood home of her great-grandfather, Karl Eschoff). She painted in Holland as well, employing models in indigenous dress, with bonnets and wooden shoes.

In those years, Louise became a woman, making her own decisions away from her father and Aunt Lizzie. She moved to different apartments in Paris, from Montparnasse, to Square de la tour Maubourg and to the Boulevard de Port-Royal. In each she would maintain a studio for painting and always a sitting room for entertaining her female friends from America.

After receiving Cousin James's moving but unexpected letter when *An Interior* was selected for the National Academy, feelings of childhood kinship developed into a trans-Atlantic romance. In letters to Aunt Lizzie, she barely hinted that James would be in New York to meet her ship when she returned from France in 1903; she suggested that Aunt Lizzie "come a few days later." To her father, Louise mentioned nothing at all about the close relationship that had grown between the two first cousins.

Louise's arrival in New York was met with mixed reactions. Frank and Emilie, with a chauffeured vehicle, were at the pier as her ship arrived. She felt their warm welcome but sensed a certain disaffection between them. And where was James, who had promised to meet her? Surely he had checked the ship's arrival time and pier number in the *Times*. What had prevented him from the reunion she expected? The answer would have to wait until later that evening.

During Louise's absence in Paris, Frank had moved his family from Brooklyn to a townhouse mansion at 620 West End Avenue, one of Manhattan's most fashionable neighborhoods. Now a horse-drawn lorry transported Louise's luggage, furniture and paintings to an apartment Frank had rented for his daughter at 49 West 69th Street, just off Central Park West and a mile south of the Dyers' residence. The large brownstone house with a wide bay window would provide abundant natural light for her painting.

Emilie had planned a formal homecoming celebration, complete with a grand dinner party, for the evening of Louise's return. Louise's three half siblings, Francis, now twenty years old and hardly a child, Frederick, fifteen, and Sarah, beautiful at fourteen, greeted their cousins James Jr. and his brother Charles. Joining the family were Grace and Constance Mills and the Nicholses and the Earles, Frank's business associates from the chemical company.

Louise hurriedly unpacked one of her steamer trunks and selected a Paris gown for the occasion. She wore the pearls and diamond ring she had bought with money sent by her father after *Le Répos* was selected for the Paris Salon.

Frank's carriage arrived for Louise at her new apartment shortly before eight for the brief drive to at the Herreshoff mansion. When she got there, waiting curbside was her cousin James. Their reunion was affectionate and demure, not attracting the notice of passersby on West End Avenue. They successfully avoided the notice of family and friends assembled in the drawing room only a few steps away as James pinned a heart-shaped diamond brooch on Louise's mauve silk gown.

Emilie had arranged the place cards on a table for fourteen in the banquet-hall-size dining room. Louise was to be seated on her father's right. Next to Louise would be James Jr., as Emilie knew her stepdaughter would have wished.

But it was not to be. Louise and James believed their three-year long-distance romance was known by no one. How wrong they were. James's brother Charles had unintentionally seen an unfinished letter from James to Louise; Emilie sensed the liaison early on when Louise never failed to mention his name in letters to her, but never in correspondence with her father; Frank took full note of James's inspired reaction to Louise's *Un Intérieur* at the opening exhibition at the National Academy.

Frank, who himself had four sightless siblings, feared that a union between Louise and her first cousin would produce blind offspring. He actively set about ending their budding romance.

Scanning the table before their guests arrived, he switched James's card with that of his brother Charles. James

would now be seated by Constance Mills rather than next to his daughter. The re-seating of guests at the dinner table foretold a series of unhappy events.

Delicate Duncan Phyfe candelabra stands, each five feet tall and with six branched taper holders, stood in the four corners of the dining room, their glow augmenting the candles in silver sticks along the length of the table. Each lady's plate held an arrangement of violets, copying the corsage in Louise's early painting *Miss T.* (plate 2). The gentlemen were presented roses for the lapels of their dinner tails.

The party, catered by Delmonico's and lasting to midnight, was a glorious affair. French wines, poured from decanters into delicate etched crystal glasses, were served by four waiters. Yet Louise and James, thinking only of each other, had little interest in the oyster bisque, wild duck, boned turkey, potato croquettes, white asparagus, brandied peaches and frozen pudding.

Conversation centered on Louise's exciting life in Paris and little of the engineering exploits of James. As glamorous and intriguing as the evening must have seemed at the time, the stage was being set for the most unfortunate years of Louise's life. When the affair ended, it was her father — not James — who escorted her home. All the while, her right hand held firmly to the diamond brooch James had given her.

Aunt Lizzie arrived in New York two days later to help Louise unpack, arrange the apartment and set up her painting studio. Frank had insisted that Louise should live in New York if she were to pursue a career in painting. New York was, after all, the center in America for arts training and exhibition. Museums, art galleries and dealers at the time paid scant atten-

OPPOSITE: LOUISE WITH THE HEART-SHAPED DIAMOND BROOCH, 1903

tion to women artists, but Frank felt strongly that his daughter could excel and overcome the profession's barriers. Yet as important as it promoting Louise's acceptance as a professional painter truly was to Frank, it was a minor consideration in comparison with his real motive: keeping Louise and James apart.

Louise confided to Aunt Lizzie her love for cousin James. Surprisingly, Lizzie offered her blessing, a blessing she gave in part because of her own painful loss of Frank when sister Grace died more than 20 years earlier. That James's father was a very wealthy inventor seemed to promise Lizzie added assurances of financial stability, although she did not mention that consideration to Louise.

As Louise settled back into life in New York, she became increasingly aware of a growing distance and aloofness between her father and stepmother at the mansion on West End Avenue. Unbeknown to her, Louise was at the center of the tension. It would be years before she learned the cause.

A marriage proposal from James had not been offered, as Louise had so desperately hoped. James was called home to California; Louise was off to Providence with Aunt Lizzie. Louise's letters went unanswered, her telephone calls unreturned. Eventually James married Constance Mills and in time they became parents to six children. Louise remained single for the next seven years, showing no desire nor, apparently, having an opportunity to marry.

CHAPTER

5

TRANSITIONS

In late 1910 Louise, at her father's urging and without Aunt Lizzie's approval, became engaged to Charles Curtis Eaton, a third cousin and also a descendant of John Brown. Charles and Louise were married on December 10 at the Herreshoffs' West End Avenue home. Emilie did not attend. Frank and Emilie for several years had hidden their marital differences, but frequent separations caused deep concern among close family members.

Lizzie attended the wedding; not so Aunt Cornelia, who stayed in Providence at the bedside of her dying sister, Lucy. Louise and Charles cancelled their honeymoon so Louise and Lizzie could be in Providence at the deathbed; Charles did not accompany them there. On New Year's Eve, the last day of 1910, Lucy died at the age of seventy-six, ending a lifetime of illness. She was buried in the Dyer vault at Mount Auburn. Sisters Lizzie and Cornelia were now alone in the Charles Field Street house.

Following Lucy's death, Louise joined Charles at their new home at 16 Waverly Place in Schenectady, New York. In February, Aunt Lizzie, bereft at losing a sister and at the same time her precious Louise, arrived for a two-week visit with the newlyweds. Almost immediately, Lizzie realized the marriage was doomed.

Charles worked long hours and often returned home late into the evening. His attempts to join Louise in the bedroom were met by a securely locked door.

The day after Lizzie left Schenectady, Louise's half-sister Sarah arrived from Italy for a short visit. The beautiful young woman, whose childhood portrait had been captured by Louise's brush in *Sarah Unfinished,* was now married to a distinguished Italian, Rudolph Borgianni, and lived in Florence. The reunion with her sister may have been the happiest moment of Louise's life in Schenectady. Sightseeing and family gossip occupied their time. Sarah was unaware of the discord surrounding her at Waverly Place. The report to her father in New York described a happy couple. Dr. Herreshoff, with good reason, suspected otherwise.

Within a month of their wedding, Charles asked his new father-in-law to place the money he had given Louise as a wedding present into a joint bank account. In the same letter, Charles complained of Louise's extravagance: She had used the wedding dowry to purchase a $5,000 diamond necklace from Cartier in New York. The remaining portion was being invested by Frank and provided $250 a month income, two and a half times Charles' monthly salary of $100. The couple agreed from the beginning to combine their monthly incomes, pay all expenses and divide equally what remained. Their expenses amounted to $150, leaving a balance of $200. Halving the $200, Charles received $100 and Louise $100. It became abundantly clear to both Louise and her father that she was providing full support for the two.

Charles' attempt to gain control of Louise's money was a continuing obsession. How best to succeed was his constant dilemma. To Aunt Lizzie, Charles wrote, "Louise is a distraught neuropath and I fear it will lead to insanity." He accused her of "dishonesty." For her part, Louise wrote to her aunt, "Charles is cruel and brutal." She accused him of "immorality."

In a desperate act, Charles attempted to have Louise hypnotized. According to Louise, he planned to force her to sign over control of her finances while she was in a hypnotic trance and subsequently have her committed to a sanitarium. The plan, undertaken less than three months into their marriage, failed when Louise contacted her father's banker and related the story to him.

After a stormy evening in March, 1911, with Charles accusing Louise of hiring a detective to report on his nightly activities, she locked the bedroom door and packed a valise. After Charles left for the office the next morning, Louise boarded a train; she was bound for Providence and Aunt Lizzie.

Her marriage to Charles Eaton had lasted ninety-six days. She never saw him again.

During the next four months, Charles wrote to his estranged wife regularly from Schenectady: "I'll be waiting for my darling at the railroad station on Saturday." The next day he would write, "My darling muffin did not come. I waited all day at the station."

His last letter was written August 29, 1911, eight months after their wedding:

> My Dear Louise:
> Your sketch and ideograph were found here on my return from out of town. The sketch breathed a spirit of loving gentle memory, but all the rest I did not understand or I hope not, unless it signifies you are well and happy.
> I have managed to keep this house open in case you should ever wish to return, Nearly all the bills, also, which your father did not pay, have been met.
> I trust you have had a pleasant summer.
>
> Yours as ever and always,
> Charles

Eight years later, on December 29, 1919, Charles Eaton would file that letter with the Superior Court of Rhode Island

and Providence Plantations, claiming as petitioner willful desertion by Louise Herreshoff Eaton for more than the five years required by law.

No response, dispute or contest of any kind was received by the court. The final decree dissolving the bond of matrimony between Charles Curtis Eaton and Louise Herreshoff Eaton was signed on July 6, 1920. Nine and a half years had passed since her wedding in New York.

During this same period, Frank divorced Mama Emilie, and in 1919 married Carrie Ridley Enslow, daughter of Dr. James Lucas Ridley of Hoboken, New Jersey. Except for occasional gifts, Frank's financial support of his children and grandchildren ended.

When Louise wrote her father for additional support, Frank, who had moved to Atlanta with his third wife, responded:

> My dear Louise:
>   Your letter of recent date received. I am glad you are well. I regret I could not come up last week. We have to consider expenses now carefully, and thought it best not to come on. I will not be able to add to your allowance at present. I hope you are all well.
>
> With love your affct. Papa,
> J.B. Francis Herreshoff

Among the Bristol Herreshoffs, it was rumored that Frank's new wife, who became an Atlanta socialite, had the major share of his considerable wealth and patent royalties placed in her own hands.

When Carrie died five years later, Frank would marry her sister, Irma Grey Ridley. In 1924 she became the fourth Mrs. J. B. Francis Herreshoff. At the time of the wedding he was seventy-five years old. The couple lived at 781 Myrtle Avenue in Atlanta, Georgia, until his death at the age of eighty-one.

The Sunday morning editions of the Atlanta *Journal* and the Atlanta *Constitution* on January 31, 1932 carried a three column obituary:

FAMED CHEMIST, J. B. F. HERRESHOFF, DIES
Noted Chemical Process Inventor, To Be Buried at Bristol.
Wealthy Research Worker retired to Atlanta Several Years Ago

A portion of the notice read:

Dr. Herreshoff made his home in New York City, removing to Atlanta in 1925. Honors bestowed upon the famous chemist included recognition from every ranking society affiliated with chemical research in America. He was a founding member and later president of the American Chemical Society, and vice-president of the Nichols Copper Company; a director of the Granby Consolidated Mining, Smelting and Power Company. The greatest honor ever awarded Dr. Herreshoff was the presentation of the Perkin Medal for outstanding achievement in the chemical-metallurgical field of endeavor, the first time the coveted award ever was made to an American scientist.

The once-close attachment between Frank and Louise had begun to wane following her return from Paris in 1903. The emotional separation widened with her divorce from Charles Eaton. Louise attended her father's funeral in 1932 at the North Burial Grounds in Bristol and there for the first time met her third stepmother. Her father's admonition to Lizzie in 1882 that Louise should always love his wife as a mother had been fulfilled through his second marriage to Emilie but not the third and fourth. There was a limit to her love beyond that given to Aunt Lizzie.

Louise remembered that upon Aunt Lizzie's death in 1927 — at the lowest period of her life — when she telegraphed her father, his fourth wife, Irma Grey Herreshoff, had acknowledged the message by sending a simple store-bought sympathy card. Fourteen years later, in 1941, Irma Grey wrote to Louise offering "motherly advice." After reading the letters, Louise tore them to pieces.

Income from the wedding gift of stocks from her father when she married Eaton and $104,000 bequeathed in his will provided Louise with ample funds to live comfortably, travel extensively, paint and pursue a new adventure: collecting antique porcelain.

After leaving Schenectady, Louise returned to Providence and Aunt Lizzie's comforting arms, room and bed. It was the familiar environment she had known from birth. Aunt Cornelia's room was down the hall.

"Release" as Louise would call it, from the mental and physical strain of her three-month marriage would permit new expressions and experiments in her works. Curiously, the signatures on her paintings carried the name "Eaton" or the initials "LHE." Even stranger, she added "Eaton" to a number of works she had painted both as a teenager and prior to her marriage in 1910. Despite the peculiar nature and brevity of their union, Louise carried his name and would have it carved on her headstone at the Dyer plot at Mount Auburn after covering the vault.

Painting and travel to resorts in the mountains and the lake country of upstate New York and to the Massachusetts and Maine coasts occupied much of Louise's time. Lizzie, usually at her side, would spend the day reading books and sewing. Tea at three o'clock was the social highlight of the day: scones with berry jams and Devonshire cream; watercress, cucumber and walnut tea sandwiches; cheese straws; lemon-ginger tea cookies and coconut macaroons; several choices of Japanese, Chinese and Indian teas. The menu would vary little from hotel to hotel, but Louise would invariably compare the setting to high tea at Brown's Hotel in London with the Aldrich family. "Not in the least comparable," she would say, remembering time and again Brown's paneled parlor, the crisp white-linen tablecloths with napkins twenty-five inches square, silver glowing from years of hand polishing, and tea cups, saucers, and tea pots of fine English Worcester or Chinese porcelain.

Louise showed her paintings at the various resorts she and Lizzie visited. Invitations to attend her exhibitions were distributed to the guests. Most of her works were marked "Not For Sale"; some carried price tags of $250. With Aunt Lizzie's help they had created a small business venture. Unfortunately there is no record of sales, but neither Louise nor Lizzie seem to have been disappointed.

In addition to upstate resort lobbies, Louise's work was seen at the Gallery on the Moors and the North Shore Art Association in Gloucester, Massachusetts, at the Rhode Island School of Design in Providence, and in Philadelphia at the Pennsylvania Academy of Fine Arts and the Philadelphia Water Color Club.

During their infrequent days apart, Lizzie's notes to Louise reported on the weather and the health of Aunt Cornelia who, unlike their late sister Lucy, was always "fit," with the exception of bouts with neuralgia.

Bridget and later Sport, the family's pet dogs, received more attention in the letters than Cornelia did. Never was a local, state, national or international political event of the day alluded to. Social invitations, though seldom accepted, were reported if descriptions could be made in one or two sentences.

The years from 1903, upon her return to America from France, until 1927 were among Louise's most unsettled. During that period she would, however, be the most productive and inventive in her painting. Art was her mate and through it, with Aunt Lizzie's love and encouragement, she would find fulfillment. It would not last.

With Louise at her side in their Charles Field Street home, Aunt Lizzie, after several weeks of illness, died the evening of

April 22, 1927. Cornelia closed the drapes on all the windows, turned off the unnecessary lights and left Louise by Lizzie's lifeless body throughout the night.

Dr. Arthur Cleves, pastor of the First Baptist Church, and Mr. Knowles, the mortician, were called early the next morning. On the fourth day after her death, Lizzie's coffin was placed in the John Dyer tomb at Mount Auburn Cemetery in Cambridge.

Louise and Aunt Cornelia returned to the Charles Field Street home after the burial. The entire house seemed to be mourning Lizzie's passing. Only Cornelia remained of the six daughters of John and Louisa Dyer. Under great physical and mental stress, Louise was determined to quit the morbid surroundings. After her treatments for mental depression at Butler Hospital, a prominent psychiatric institution, she bought and remodeled her future home at 93 Benevolent. Cornelia would have her own room, but only briefly; she died the following year at age 86. Her casket would be the last to be interred in the tomb at Mount Auburn Cemetery. The tomb had reached its capacity.

Louise, alone in the house, would occupy the room dedicated to Aunt Lizzie. Furnishings at 93 Benevolent were situated as closely as possible to the arrangement at Charles Field Street. Louise's life of art, along with tubes of colored oils, watercolor boxes, brushes and palettes were locked away in the attic.

Louise lost all incentive to paint and, for a while, all will to live.

◆

CHAPTER

6

A CHANCE ENCOUNTER

Ear-piercing sounds coming from the remodeling of the frame house being encased with brick, stone, slate, copper and steel at 93 Benevolent Street in Providence contrasted sharply with the dreamy big-band chords heard 600 miles away at Washington and Lee University in Lexington, Virginia.

In Rhode Island, Louise Herreshoff Eaton was keeping a watchful eye on each step of the builders' progress, giving one change order after another. In Virginia, Euchlin Dalcho Reeves Jr. danced with his date to Jan Garber's fifteen-piece orchestra at the Finals Ball and at the *dansant* at the Pi Kappa Phi fraternity house.

Activities north and south were poles apart. Nothing in either place on that warm June day in 1927 foretold the convergence of Louise's and Euchlin's lives fourteen years later.

It was in that year of 1927 that Louise, upon her return to health at Butler Hospital, learned that the Charles Field Street home, rented by the Dyer family for nearly a century, had been put up for sale. The Charles F. Hunter Real Estate Company gave Louise first option to buy, but she declined to meet the owners' price. A nearby property at 93 Benevolent Street offered an affordable challenge with the opportunity to incorporate privacy, security and architectural features she

WASHINGTON COLLEGE, C. 1840,
WHICH BECAME WASHINGTON AND LEE UNIVERSITY IN 1871

THE SECOND BUILDING FROM THE RIGHT WOULD LATER BECOME HOME
TO THE REEVES COLLECTION

had seen during her travels abroad. The wedding present of stocks and bonds given by her father at the time of the ill-fated marriage to Charles Eaton had appreciated greatly and would provide ample funds to undertake the transformation of the house from frame to brick.

Meanwhile, in the small Shenandoah Valley town of Lexington, Euchlin Reeves — Euc or Euchie to his friends — and his law school classmates joined in all the festivities being enjoyed by the graduating seniors. The college newspaper, *The Ring-tum Phi,* reported: "With the arrival of friends, sweethearts and families, the thoughts of responsibilities temporarily suspended from the mind, came the invincible desire for gaiety and pleasure."

One hundred nine undergraduate liberal-arts and science degrees and twenty-seven bachelor of law degrees would be conferred by the college president, Henry Louis Smith. Finals ceremonies lasted from June 3 to June 7. Attendance by the graduates was required at the baccalaureate sermon on Sunday morning, the fifth, but few of the graduates would recall the minister's sermon. In addition to a small number of faculty and the families of the graduates, only a handful of students were counted at vesper services at six o'clock on Sunday evening.

Euc was one of the many absentees. Along with his date and most of his fellow graduates, he was a few miles north of Lexington at Goshen Pass, one of nature's most beautiful mountain retreats. The normally placid run of the Maury River was made turbulent and icy by winter's melting snow; picnic and party areas bordered the rocky banks.

Unlike most of his brethren with out-of-town dates, Euc would escort to all the parties for three days of revelry his true first love, a charming belle who attended Hollins College, about fifty miles to the southwest but whose family lived in Lexington a few doors away from his fraternity house in

EUCHLIN REEVES, WASHINGTON AND LEE UNIVERSITY
FRONT CAMPUS, 1927

THE BUILDING OVER HIS LEFT SHOULDER
LATER WOULD BECOME THE REEVES CENTER

an imposing red-brick antebellum home. Their relationship, with a mutual interest in music, social gaiety and Old Gold cigarettes, had grown close since he arrived from Atlanta. Her father, a Washington and Lee administrator, did not share his daughter's exuberance for young Mr. Reeves.

Study at Piedmont Academy in Demorest, Georgia, had prepared Euc for undergraduate study at Emory University. His parents, Chester Green Raiford of Milledgeville, Georgia, and Euchlin D. Reeves Sr. of Orangeburg, South Carolina, had been married in 1891. In partnership with a relative, Dr. A. C. Dukes, Mr. Reeves Sr. operated the Dukes and Reeves Crockery and Fine China Store in Orangeburg, where the Reeveses' three sons, Winfield R. (Robbie), Chester (named for his mother) and Euc, were born. Robbie attended the Citadel; Chester, the College of Charleston; and Euc, Emory and Washington and Lee. Despite personal sacrifice, the Reeveses were determined that, even during the Depression, each son would receive a college education.

Following her husband's death in 1922, Mrs. Reeves owned and operated a resort hotel, the Mountain View, in Clarkesville, Georgia. Later it would become the home of an antiques business run by Euc and brother Chester.

In Providence, Louise, slowly but with inherited Prussian determination, overcame her mental collapse after the death of Aunt Lizzie. She regained her health, spent untold sums of money on the renovation of 93 Benevolent, and eventually emerged from the cocoon she had spun.

She began traveling again in the United States and across western Europe. Each city on her tour provided exciting finds as she became an avid collector of antique porcelain. She and her wealthy friends — Louise seemed to have no other kind — found great satisfaction in the pursuit of the old and the beautiful. Lucy Aldrich, her friend from years past in Europe, was her guide as Louise concentrated on eighteenth-century German ceramics. A large Meissen platter that she had purchased years before during her travels with her art teacher, Mary Wheeler, set the standard for the beauty and rarity she now sought. She accumulated items with eighteenth-century marks from porcelain factories in Berlin, Vienna, Hochst, Ludwigsburg and Nymphenburg from dealers and collectors as she traveled in America and abroad.

Euc, after graduating, did not enter the practice of law but instead accepted a sales position with the Balfour College Jewelry Company, whose headquarters happened to be in Rhode Island. A hale fellow well met, he seemed tailor-made for a sales position on college campuses up and down the East Coast. On party weekends, merchandise in hand, he gravitated from one fraternity house to the next. Capitalizing on his musical and dramatic talents, Euc drew students and their dates around the piano through the force of his magnetic personality. He played and sang their favorite tunes, eliciting gales of laughter when the lyrics turned risqué. When the party reached full pitch, Euc would open his collapsible display case, and the gold and pearl pins and bracelets with each fraternity's Greek insignia flashed before cloudy eyes. How could any brother resist such a gift for his beloved?

By no means as famous as Jan Garber, Euc nevertheless became liked and admired in the select world he traveled. The word would spread: "Euchie Reeves will be at the Sigma house on Friday afternoon and the Beta house on Saturday night." His work, often requiring late-night partying, was profitable but physically demanding. Though he was still young, Euc's nascent career began to take its toll, and gradually the life of a traveling salesman gave way to other endeavors. His greatest loss would be that of his college sweetheart, the result of her father's resistance. She remained unmarried throughout her life as Euc's proposals of matrimony went unheeded.

By 1930, Euc had returned to north Georgia and joined his brother Chester in the small antiques shop at the Mountain View. His interest in eighteenth- and nineteenth-century American decorative arts came from the influence of his mother, who acquired old and beautiful furniture and used it to furnish her Mountain View Hotel. The antiques enterprise, in one form or another, would continue for years.

A major change in Euc's professional career came four years after his Washington and Lee days when he joined an exciting new venture with his cousin, Hazard E. "Buz" Reeves, a distinguished engineering graduate of Atlanta's Georgia Tech.

The Atlanta *Journal* in full-page coverage on April 7, 1935, headlined the story:

Georgians Make Noise Pay

The Reeves cousins, Bzz and Euc, of Atlanta and Clarkesville, make phonograph records and provide sound for silent movies in their New York studio. Adding dialogue to Chinese pictures and giving realistic effects to war scenes are among the tough problems they have solved.

In their studio sixteen stories above Broadway, the cousins made phonograph records and electrical transcriptions for radio and screen stars, and supplied sound continuities for motion pictures. Eleanor Roosevelt, Fannie Hurst, Amelia Earhart, Joe Penner, Lowell Thomas, Bing Crosby and the Pickens Sister of Georgia were among their clients. Buz was the engineer, and Euc the salesman.

Buz would go on to form several successful media enterprises, including one that developed Cinerama, a seven-track sound system that gave the illusion of depth and dimension to a massive concave screen; he would also own several radio and television stations. The capstone of his successful and lucrative career came with special recognition by the Academy of Motion Picture Arts and Sciences, which awarded him an honorary Oscar, and the Society of Motion Picture and Television Engineers.

Euc's peripatetic nature, combined with an innate desire to lead, not follow, and with a moderate intemperance for intoxicants since college days, led to the dissolution of his intertwined business associations with cousin Hazard. It was a step he regretted at times: He found himself missing the glamour and financial reward. Euc eventually sold his stock in the company.

Early in 1940 Euc traveled to Rhode Island, hoping to renew his association with Balfour there. The timing was inopportune, as war in Europe and mobilization of America's young men depleted the nation's collegiate fraternities. Instead, he accepted an administrative position with the Goodyear Tire Company.

His continuing interest in collecting and selling fine antiques brought him in touch with like-minded people in Providence. In the South, great quantities of decorative pieces had been destroyed during the Civil War. But in the Northeast, barely scarred since the American Revolution, the finest examples of eighteenth- and nineteenth-century furniture, silver, porcelain and beaux arts were abundant. In many cases the objects had descended from and were still in the possession of families of the original owners.

Thus it was that Louise Herreshoff Eaton and Euchlin Dalcho Reeves met in early 1941, brought together by their mutual interest in and passion for seeking out and acquiring antiques: she for the rare and beautiful, he for the old and historic, at times interchangeable. The two sat next to each other at the winter meeting of the Providence Pottery and Porcelain Club. He was the guest of another collector, the afternoon's featured speaker. "Chinoiserie and Chinese Porcelain for the Rhode Island Home" was the topic. John Brown and his three ships named for George Washington were mentioned prominently. Little did Euc know that Brown's great-great granddaughter was seated in the ballroom chair on his right.

At the social gathering that followed the address, Euc met Mrs. Eaton over a cup of tea and quickly learned of her Brown family ancestry. Louise met a true gentleman with southern manners and knowledge of American antiques. Reserved and shy, Louise happily allowed the magnetic Mr. Reeves to dominate the conversation, his jovial personality suited to the group environment. More than a little to the chagrin of the club's president, members began a natural gravitation to the charming and new Mr. Reeves, and were soon ignoring the afternoon's featured speaker.

Euc had arrived and was quickly accepted into that rarified segment of Providence society. Invitations to luncheons, dinners and other social events soon followed. Louise was always included among the guests, and in time Euc became her escort. There was never a lack of shared conversation, as the subject of period furniture and other antiques resurrected memories for both. When the conversation changed, genealogy filled the void, each attempting to outdo the other.

Louise and Euc, on a Sunday afternoon drive, headed for Bristol to visit her nephew, Norman Herreshoff, and her second cousin, Louise DeWolf. On arriving at Hope Street near Burnside, she asked Euc to stop the car. Nearby was a large frame house, rich ivory in color, overlooking the bay: the home in which her father and his eight brothers and sisters were born.

Neither Louise nor Euc ever described the moment of joy they shared along the shore of Narragansett Bay, where much of Louise's history seemed alive. George Washington, following the Revolutionary War, had made property available to John Brown across Bristol Harbor on Poppasquash Point. This confiscated estate had belonged to a Tory, William Vassal, until the end of the war. John Brown's daughter Sarah would inherit the land and buildings after his death in 1803. She and

LOUISE HERRESHOFF EATON, 1941
(ARTIST UNKNOWN)

Left: plate, bearing the insignia of the Society of the Cincinnati, made for George Washington; Qianlong, China, c. 1785. Right: guglet with the Lee family coat of arms; Yongzheng, China, c. 1733

Dish with orange Fitzhugh border and patriotic decoration; Jiaqing, China, c. 1810-20

All pieces from the Reeves Center, Washington and Lee University
Photos by Ellen Martin

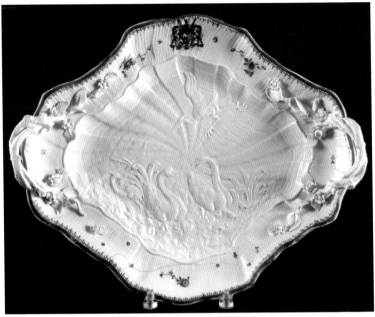

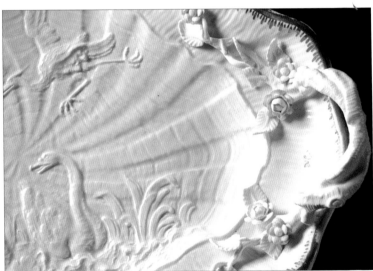

Tray and detail from the "Swan
Service," made by order of Augustus
III; Meissen, Germany, 1737-1741

Saltglaze enameled "King of Prussia" teapot and cover, with decoration celebrating Frederick II (Frederick the Great), great-nephew of King George I of England; Staffordshire, England, 1757-60. Louise Herreshoff's great-grandfather Karl Frederich Eschoff was a favorite of the king, in whose court he was raised.

Drum-shaped teapot with crossed handles and bell-shaped sugar bowl, both with strawberry knops and decorated with thick blue enamel and gold accents; Qianlong/Jiaqing, China, c. 1790-1805

Bowl decorated in polychrome enamels and gold, showing the "hongs" (trade offices) on the waterfront at Canton showing the American and other flags; Qianlong/Jiaqing, c. 1790-1802

Above: plate decorated en grisaille and in gold, showing the Nativity; Qianlong, China, c. 1750

Right: plate in polychrome enamels, showing Don Quixote; Qianlong, China, c. 1742

her husband, Karl Frederich Herreschoff, married in 1801 and made Poppasquash their home. Louise did not mention that Karl committed suicide in the Adirondack Mountains after years of attempting to bring profit to land that belonged to his father-in-law.

Of their six children, only Charles would marry, and he moved across the harbor to Bristol. With his wife, Julia Ann Lewis, they raised the "Amazing Nine," of whom John Brown Francis, Louise's father, was one. Louise inherited a small portion of the income from the sale of Poppasquash after her father's generation had passed on. And so it went, always good-naturedly but always speaking of the past, either antiques or ancestry. That world was long gone, but Louise and Euc treasured its history.

Three months had passed since the Pottery and Porcelain Club meeting in February, and each day brought the pair's attachment closer. During the blossoming romance an unexpected postcard arrived from Louise's cousin — and unrequited lover — James. The card reflected gossip from parlors in Bristol and along Benevolent, Waterman, Williams and Benefit Streets in Providence:

March 11, 1941

Dear Louise:

This is blizzard day eve. Fred Herreshoff [a first cousin] was also born March 11, 1888. We heard Hoffman at Carnegie Hall last Saturday. He played the Revolutionary etude beautifully and also like a very angry person. I wish you had been with us. I have been trying to have the U.S. Steel Corporation adopt one of my furnaces. It will be wonderful if they take it. You live too far away in that cold snowy Providence. I have been playing Bach's D minor fugue arranged for the piano by Tausig. It is très difficile. When at the piano I always think of you, which is every day. With much love I am your affectionate cousin.

J. B. H.

The message stirred memories of James, family reunions in Bristol as a small child, the bench at the old Herreshoff piano, James's letters when she lived in Paris. Memories too of his marriage to Constance and the years of silence were recalled. But after the long period of her unhappiness, she could now erase those thoughts from her mind.

The card from James came after Euc and Louise had given subtle hints to friends and relatives in Rhode Island, South Carolina and Georgia of an impending engagement. The news spread fast in Providence.

In April, Louise acknowledged James's card, and he answered with a rather unromantic message:

> The U.S. Steel did not do anything favorable so I am now trying the Bethlehem Steel Corporation. My furnace is beautiful but it is so unlike other steel furnaces that ordinary people are inclined not to bother with it.
>
> I wish I could see you. If you could put me up over night I could get my Studebaker car ready for a trip to Providence. It would be magnificent if you would come to New York. The Germans are devils. With lots of love I am your very affectionate cousin.

J. B. H.

In early May Euc proposed to Louise, a short three months after their introduction, and she accepted immediately. Euc purchased from the Providence jeweler Tilden-Thurber a wedding band of small diamonds. Louise and Euc chose Thursday, May 29, 1941, for their wedding date, with the ceremony to be performed at St. John's Chancery by the Right Reverend James De Wolfe Perry, Bishop of Rhode Island.

Louise wrote immediately to Julia Herreshoff, a cousin living in Bristol:

A CHANCE ENCOUNTER

May 15, 1941

Dear Julia,

I was very sorry you were not feeling well the day I called on you with Mr. Reeves. I wanted you to meet him, as he has now become my fiancé. I met him sometime ago at the Pottery and Porcelain Club and we are to be married the twenty-ninth of this month, very privately by Bishop Perry.

Perhaps you will be so kind as to tell . . . other members of the family.

Everyone will have an announcement card of course. With love and hoping that you are feeling stronger.

Affectionately,
Louise Herreshoff Eaton

Louise wrote to cousins of the Dyer side of her family in Boston, and Euc wrote his South Carolina and Georgia relatives. The Dyer and Reeves families would send positive responses; not so for the Herreshoffs.

From a cousin in Brookline, Massachusetts, the note read: "Just read the exciting news of your approaching marriage. May you both live a long and happy life together."

Another Dyer cousin wrote:

Here comes another exclamation. Yes, it was a great surprise and I send all good wishes that every happiness may be yours. It will be wonderful to have companionship and I am keen to meet the fortunate man. Heartfelt congratulations.

P.S. You are a most surprising lady!

From Chester, Euc's brother, on May 18th:

My dear Louise,

Just a few lines to wish you well and much happiness. We will be delighted to have you in our family and I do want you and Euchie to stay at my house while in Clarkesville. If you feel so disposed, do write us your plans as when to expect you both, by rail or motor?

Yours most Sincerely and Cordially.
J. Chester Reeves.

A FRAGILE UNION

Sisterly advice came from a Boston cousin:

Dear Louise,
 It was so lovely to see you and meet Euch. We all like him so much and I do hope you will have a very happy time together. I do hope you will have your rooms upstairs in order. Be sure the beds are all made before you leave on your wedding trip. You do not want your husband, to see that nothing had been done for his comfort. He certainly is so kind and devoted. Don't let him know I have been giving you advice. We want him to be very happy and comfortable.
 My love and best wishes to the bride of "Sweet Sixteen."

Letters began arriving at 93 Benevolent at a frenetic pace. Louise, caught up in the details of preparation for her wedding, had the time to read only a few. Thirty-eight years had passed — thirty-eight years of sadness, the miserable marriage to Charles Eaton, illness and loneliness. The last three months, with her life changed after meeting Euchlin Reeves, caused Louise a momentary, somewhat trite thought: "Where were they during all those dark and empty days?"

More important were the arrangements for the 29th of May; the wedding trip, the reservations, the printed announcements, the preparation of the rooms at 93, her wedding and travel wardrobe. So much to do — and Euc was busier than ever at Goodyear. It was a time of pressure the bride-to-be had not known for many years. Close friends of Louise arranged special prenuptial events. The Vernons' dinner, a luncheon at the Dwights', a party at the Howarths' — all of it kept the pair on the go the weeks before the wedding.

Louise would hear from the fourth Mrs. J. B. Francis Herreshoff, her third stepmother. The letter was the first communication since her father's will had become known nine years before. Motherly advice, at this time of her life, was of no interest to Louise.

A CHANCE ENCOUNTER

Dear Louise:

Of course I am very much surprised at the announcement of your engagement and I wish you had written me your intentions before you took such a decided adventure at your time of life.

I feel the deepest motherly interest in you in this very serious step in your life. First you did not tell me this man's name, which I want to know. Is he a man of position in the business world and has he a settled position to take care of you?

The majority of men who would marry a woman older than themselves, generally marry them so that they may be taken care of and as a rule desert them in later years for younger women. I want you to ponder all of these questions before you take this step, for it is not to late. I worked very hard over Dr. Herreshoff's money, to save a nice living for each and all of you [Louise, Sarah and Norman], and I want you to be assured of that through life.

Remember a man has quite a legal right over your affairs after a ceremony is pronounced. Write me by return mail this man's name and something of his ability to take care of you and yours. This is all from my deep interest and love for you for I feel you have so few to advise you. Sarah's address as given me by Mr. Beatty in 1934 is Mrs. Rudolph F. Borgianni, Viale Macchiavella 4, Florence, Italy.

I have thought so often of Sarah in this late war and wondered if her boys have been in the Army, as so many Italian youths have been sacrificed for nothing.

Now write me at once of your plans and believe all that I have said is from love of you.

Lovingly,
Mother Grey

Crossing letters in the mail would bring cousin Julia Herreshoff a most disturbing note from Louise's latest stepmother in Atlanta. Irma Grey spelled out her concern of the union and especially of the intended groom.

Dear Julia:

A week or ten days ago I received a short note from Louise with the amazing announcement of her marriage on May 29th by Bishop Perry, not telling me the man's name but that she would visit Atlanta as she would be visiting this man's brother at Clarkesville, Ga., a very small town near Atlanta.

From another source, and a clue of his brother living in Clarkesville, I located this man and immediately had the wires busy as to his identification.

His name is Euchlin D. Reeves. He has had the advantages of education. Graduated at our Emory University, a University of high standing, also a post-graduate course at Washington and Lee. He had a position as manager of a Tire Co. — but did not keep it, and since collected antiques. I presume he cannot keep any position on account of his intemperance. As the report was he kept sober two weeks and [not] the third.

I feel that Louise is such a helpless little woman she needs the advice and protection of the Herreshoffs, as she knows so little of the world, and designing men. Of course the only conclusion and answer to a man about 35 — marrying a woman Louise's age — that it is for some ulterior motive and for her money.

I worked so hard over Dr. Herreshoff's money so the heirs would have a living and it would make me very happy for Louise to marry a man near her age, sober and industrious and make a home for her.

Do you know if she was divorced from Mr. Eaton, if so Bishop Perry would not marry a divorced woman — it is contrary to the laws of the Episcopal Church. If she has no proof of his death, she could not marry any man.

Please call Norman and if there is any way possible to prevent this marriage for I have her deepest welfare at heart and as you know no other motive.

I hope your health is better and remember me to Anne and Norman.

With love,
Irma Grey

A CHANCE ENCOUNTER

Irma Grey sent a similar letter to Louise:

Dear Louise:

Possibly this is the last letter you will ever receive from me if you do not reconsider and give up the fatal mistake you are making in marrying Mr. Euchlyn *[sic]* D. Reeves of Clarkesville, Ga. In writing me, you did not tell me his name but the world is small and I have found out all about this man. He has had the advantages of a good education, a graduate of Emory University here in Atlanta. Then he had a post-graduate course at Washington & Lee.

That shows [it could have] been the foundation for a proper business career. He had a good position with a tire company but did not hold it; I suppose the result of intemperance. I was told he was sober two weeks and [not] the week afterwards. And of course no man can hold any position under such circumstances. After he lost that job he collected antiques — I presume that association which led him to you — as the Herreshoffs are known to have [fine] antiques. I hear he is now selling auto tires in Providence.

Of course Louise, I have no other interest at heart but your welfare and nothing would give me more happiness than for you to find companionship in a good, sober man near your age of good position and dependable. But for you to marry a dissipated man with no past, present or future and half your age is an impossible situation.

Remember you have no good father to appeal to if your money is dissipated, and as for myself I am through. I will change my will and you will not be mentioned and mark and digest what I have written and realize that a man about 35 who marries a woman about 65 is marrying for some ulterior motive, not for love for it is contrary to nature.

I am with love,
Mother Grey

Irma Grey Herreshoff's letters to Louise promised disinheritance if she married Euc Reeves; Louise ripped them up. Where had Irma Grey been when Louise asked her father for financial help before his death in 1932?

Accustomed to being the last to know of the dramas that shaped her life, none would compare to the letter of May 20 from her first cousin, Charles Herreshoff, written on behalf of his brother James. It would bring to her the unhappy memory of her return to New York from France in 1903 with the hope of marrying James.

May 20, '41

Dear Louise,
    Thirty-eight years ago your father related to me how your mother died in childbirth. Your mother was his first and only love and remained so! He really never got over it and with tears in his eyes remarked that her death was due to narrow hips. He felt that you inherited your narrow hips from her and therefore did not wish you to marry and suffer the same fate. He enlisted my support and we both worked on [brother] James to that end. He [Frank Herreshoff] found somewhere in N.Y. a "wild ass" of the Golden West and paraded her virtues before James constantly. Particularly her musical ability, Jim's one weakness. The devilish scheme worked! Your two lives were sacrificed. Oh, how much sweeter life would have been for you had it failed. My part in it? Every time you or your aunt would call on the phone from Prov. to N.Y. I made it my point and duty to your father's wishes to say, "Jim is out of town — sorry!" It was all done as we thought for the best.
    What damned fools mortals can be! I didn't know much about complexes then — I do now, and of course the terrible physical and mental suffering your mother Grace went through printed a picture that never could be erased from your father's mind. That explains it but doesn't correct the sad mistake. It seems that you alone can do just that! It takes character! It take guts! You know that Jim has always loved you and that really there never could be anyone but you. He has been suffering all through his married adventure; his very heart longing for you — torn to shreds by emotion.
    I know he went east to see you and now my sister writes that you intend to marry a much younger man the twenty-ninth of this month. Let me remind you as one who has succeeded in this life to snatching some happiness out of it that thirty-eight years of love and devotion, however little allowed to be expressed will never give way to an infatuation dressed up by wishful thinking to represent love. No it just won't work; it only spells unhappiness — sorry, but true every time! I don't

believe in beating about the bush on any matter; it is a waste of time and energy. I believe in and have proved it the only way was to cut the dog's tail off once and in the right place. I do not believe, and I have proved this too, is that weakness to make a just and proper decision means cutting the dog's tail off by inches until the right place is reached causing much unnecessary pain and killing the dog!

Reno is a delightful place this time of year. Why not pack your little bag, go to N.Y., get Jim, and motor West, quietly, decisive and go thru with it — one week to get there and six to put it through; and heaven on earth thereafter! Why not?

Well it takes character — a lot of it. It takes guts! But anything in this world that is worthwhile takes both. The question is, have you got it? You have if you let your head rule and your spirit lead — a difficult thing to do, but all worthwhile things are difficult, the bitter must come before the sweet; we want the sweet to be last and linger on; it must be so! But if the flesh is too weak and the mind and spirit can't lead; then for God's sake let consideration rule apace; postpone your wedding a month and give Jim a chance to collect himself. But I'll meet you in Reno, that's the way — the only lasting way to happiness and Jim is receptive.

In haste but very affectionately yours,
Charles

In the same mail were two letters from James; both were postmarked before the California letter from Charles Herreshoff but both arrived after it. James professed his love and his concern if Louise were to marry Euc. His letter of May 20, written from San Diego, did not propose marriage as his brother Charles had done for him:

. . . I have had such a terrible time for ten years that I sometimes cannot control my emotions. Dear sweet Louise believe me you are not badly off the way you are. You have all your senses unimpaired. You have good health, and you have security. You said to me that I could not understand what it was to be lonely. The most lonely people in the world are those that because of defective hearing cannot enter into general conversation. Your status is so good that you would not improve it by making an alliance with one vastly inferior to you in mental equipment. The sting of neglect can be many times as painful as that of loneliness. You can reckon it as true that the young man is worthless who shirks his duties to society and to his country and tries to win his board and lodging by the easy way of marriage to an elderly lady. In my own case I would be afraid to contract an alliance with a young woman. The world has a greater contempt by far for the male gold digger than for his sister.

I do not know why my affection for you increases with the years. Perhaps it is because an old person does not make new friends easily and therefore clings to the friends of his youth. You were certainly the sweetest, the dearest, and the most inspiring friend of my youth, but now you are even more so.

With lots of love I am your affectionate cousin,

James B. Herreshoff

James' second letter professed his love again:

Dear Sweet Louise:

Your letter which you dated May 22 came Saturday Noon, May 17. It gave me a terrible shock and ever since I have an empty feeling in the vicinity of my stomach.

Please do not say that I look down on your intelligence. On the contrary I love you so much because you are the most intelligent person that I have ever known. But when love and passion enter the picture, reason suffers an eclipse for a short period just as the moon hides the face of the sun for a few minutes every year. Your father was a very intelligent man yet at the sight of Carrie Ridley his intelligence waned to such an extent that he turned over to her all his wealth and allowed his helpless children to be disinherited. It has always been so since the beginning of the world. The ancient Greeks maintained that Venus was the most powerful of all the gods. She certainly made a fool of Jupiter.

Dear Louise, great harm can come to you by being unnecessarily hasty in this matter. Irma Grey has about half a million dollars which she promised me would go to your father's children. She will certainly disinherit you if you take this step without consulting her. I knew in San Diego a beautiful widow with a very wealthy mother-in-law. A very nice man who later became a judge courted her and asked her to be his wife. Before accepting him she sent him to her mother-in-law to be looked over. As a result the mother was so pleased with the man that she told her daughter that if she did not marry him quickly she would marry him herself. The marriage took place very soon and all three plus a baby lived in a very congenial atmosphere.

Dear Louise you can be wise also. Please do these things. Put off your wedding for a few days. Write to Irma Grey telling her about your plans and asking her advice and offering to send the young man to Atlanta so that she can look him over and pass on him.

2. See your doctor for a personal examination and advice to prepare you and fit you for the additional stress that will be put upon your system.

3. Have the young man go to your doctor for personal examination. It is absolutely important that it is your doctor who makes the examination and his report must go to you directly. A report from his doctor will not do.

In your letter you suggest that I could have a little of your love if I want it. Of course you must know that I want and need all the love that you will give me. We would have been married 38 years ago had it not been for the great fear of having blind babies. I have never mentioned this subject to anyone. For the great love that you once had for me please do the things that I have requested if not for your own welfare.

I wish you would make us your promised visit or invite me to visit you. I could go to Providence in my little car and bring you back in it to New York if you wish. Please know that I shall always love you never mind what happens. Again with all the love that you want to keep I am ever your affectionate cousin.

James B. Herreshoff

Anticipating the very special event on May 29, 1941, and his marriage to Louise, Euc had written in his date book "The greatest and happiest event in my life."

On the appointed day, the Clarkesville, Georgia, *Tri-County Advertiser* published this story:

Mrs. Louise H. Eaton,
Euchlin D. Reeves, Jr. to
Wed in Providence, R.I.

An announcement of interest to a wide circle of friends is that of the engagement of Mrs. Louise Herreshoff Eaton, of Providence, R.I. to Euchlin Dalcho Reeves, Jr. of Providence and Clarkesville, which appeared in a recent newspaper of that place.

The wedding is scheduled to take place today, Thursday, May 29, at high noon in St. John's Chancery, the ceremony to be performed by Rt. Rev. James De Wolfe Perry, Bishop of Rhode Island.

Mrs. Eaton is the daughter of the late James Brown Francis Herreshoff.

Mr. Reeves is the son of the late Euchlin Dalcho Reeves and Chester Raiford Green Reeves, prominent residents of Clarkesville for a number of years and formerly of Orangeburg, S.C. He is a graduate of Washington and Lee University and a member of Pi Kappa Phi Fraternity.

Mr. Reeves holds an executive position with the Goodyear Tire Company and has been located at Providence, R.I. for the past year.

By the time it was published, however, the front-page notice was two days late. The wedding had already taken place forty-eight hours earlier. But why the sudden change in plans?

On May 27, in a mid-morning telephone call from New York, cousin James threatened Louise and warned her not to marry Euchlin Reeves. Frightened by James' message, she quickly went to Euc's office at the Goodyear Company. She and Euc contacted Bishop Perry, and it was agreed the wedding would be held that very evening. No one else was told.

Louise Eaton and Euchlin Reeves eloped two days before the original date they had set to marry. The wedding ring was still at the Tilden-Thurber jewelry store, and the wedding ensemble had yet to arrive from Boston. A Providence florist hurriedly arranged six crimson roses in a nosegay — the only sign of the upcoming evening marriage at nine o'clock at St. John's Episcopal Church in Barrington, Rhode Island. The Reverend Richard Maddox presided; the Bishop was not in evidence. Anne T. Vernon, Field Secretary of the Diocese, was witness.

Anne Vernon's letter to the Rev. Maddox explained the dilemma:

To: The Reverend Richard Maddox

Dear Mr. Maddox:

I am terribly sorry that there has been so much trouble and misunderstanding about Mrs. Eaton's marriage and that you should have to bear the brunt of it.

Bishop Perry sent me a copy of the letter he wrote you and I cannot quite understand his attitude.

In the first place he said he wanted to see me, which he did for a few moments. Said he wanted to see me again which he did not do, though I made several unsuccessful attempts to get an appointment.

Will you please read the enclosed letter, which Mrs. Eaton asked Adelaide to show the Bishop. When she did he said it threw another light on the story. Mrs. Eaton rightfully I think refused to see Mr. James Herreshoff alone and Adelaide herself heard him say to her "You've got to see me or it will be the worse for you." Both she and her friend began to feel she was not safe in Providence. Bishop Perry told Mr. Reeves and Mrs. Eaton to come to him as soon as they got the license, which they did Tues. and they immediately came to the office with it but the Bishop had gone to Princeton (RI) and Miss Johnson told them they could see him at his house between 8 and 10 in the evening. They telephoned for an appt. only to find he had unexpectedly gone to New York by boat instead of by the midnight train as they had been told. When all this trouble developed they simply did not dare wait.

We were not responsible for your being called but after consulting a Providence Clergyman, we decided that the situation was such as to make a justifiable exception, and then the Bishop had had more than a three-day notice.

LOUISE AND EUCHLIN ELOPED TO BARRINGTON, R.I.,
AND WERE MARRIED AT ST. JOHN'S EPISCOPAL CHURCH
ON THE EVENING OF MAY 27, 1941

Evidently there was a misunderstanding all round, but I hate to have you involved for there is no clergyman in R.I. that I respect or admire more, but when ever I think of the beautiful service you had I feel as if all the difficulties and mistakes must have been ironed out.

Gratefully yours.
Anne T. Vernon

P.S. In regard to Mrs. Eaton's mental condition, Dr. Westcott of Butler Hospital gave her a "clean bill of mental health" on which the granting of a marriage license depended and what was most surprising was that the man that made all the trouble about it being wrong for her to marry, wished to marry her himself. Yet, let his brother make the proposal about marrying her after he got the divorce. As the two parties were both of age and pronounced by the psychiatrist to be of sound mind, I do not see that any of us could do anything to stop the marriage. Mrs. Eaton is odd and eccentric but my sister had a happy time traveling round the world with her. Mrs. Eaton had a bad nervous breakdown after a great sorrow had come into her life, which was the reason of her being in Butler Hospital. Forgive errors as I have had to write in haste and it was difficult to explain the situation.

The wedding trip and the honeymoon advanced by two days took them by automobile first to Williamsburg, Virginia, then to Charlotte, North Carolina, and to meet relatives and friends in Orangeburg, South Carolina, and Clarkesville, Georgia. The warmth and hospitality of the Reeves family was so unfamiliar to Louise she felt as though she were in a foreign country. She loved every minute and her innate shyness gave way to obvious pleasure. She gave no thought to the disinheritance by her stepmother.

Louise and Euc's years together forged an even stronger bond around their mutual interest in antiques, especially porcelain and furniture. Dealers throughout the east came to know them as a loving and gracious couple, highly knowledgeable but never ostentatiously so.

In 1953 they sailed aboard the *HMS Queen Elizabeth* for a tour of the European continent. They visited sites Louise had frequented as an art student with Mary Wheeler more than fifty years before. An abundance of German and English porcelain was added to their ever-expanding collection. The highlight of the trip came with their stay in London during the coronation of Elizabeth II.

They relived their journey many times as items they had purchased abroad continued to arrive for months after their return to 93 Benevolent Street. They eagerly unwrapped, admired and researched the contents of every new shipment. Each delicate piece was placed atop another, and they never touched most of them again.

The collection soon outgrew the confines of 93 Benevolent, so the Reeveses purchased the small frame house next door at 89 and moved into it. Leaving their collection at 93, they dedicated that house as their "little museum." New purchases were placed in the museum and in the stone vaults at the rear which Louise had added at the time of the renovation. Euc, after returning from their wedding journey, found that matters related to collecting and, later, caring for Louise consumed most of his time. He resigned his position with Goodyear and devoted himself full time to developing the collection and serving on Rhode Island's civil defense councils and as class agent for the Washington and Lee University law class of 1927.

Many of those who had expressed concern, both publicly and privately, about Louise's decision to marry Euchlin soon changed their minds. Those who knew the couple accepted Euc and admired him for the love and care he exhibited during their marriage — excepting only Mother Irma.

Euc's marriage to Louise, which some felt was for love and money, but not necessarily in that order, was undoubtedly a fragile union. It was a union of contrasts: of ages mature and young, of financial wealth and moderate means, and of personal shyness and ebullience. The fragility of the marriage was no less than that of the rare and delicate porcelains they handled each day. However strange the beginning may have seemed, the questioning thoughts disappeared from the minds of most. The Reeveses would reach the year of their silver wedding anniversary; it was a milestone of strong and enduring attachment following their elopement when Louise was sixty-six and Euc was thirty-eight.

◆

CHAPTER

7

A POSTCARD PURSUED

The unanticipated moment had arrived when we were to come face to face. In fact, I never expected to meet Louise Herreshoff Reeves. The image of Mrs. Reeves that had formed in my mind's eye since meeting her husband three years earlier had been painted by the descriptive words of others. My perception was completely transformed, however, in her room at Ruth's Nursing Home, 26 Fourth Street in East Providence, Rhode Island. The date was January 12, 1967, the day before her husband was to be buried.

The home was a converted, two-story white frame residence in a working-class neighborhood of first-, second- and third-generation immigrants. Anchored in the deep snow and ice, the façade was bleak and foreboding. But its starkness gave way to warmth when we passed through the front door and met Ruth Lama, the cheerful proprietress and head nurse. The small group there included Donald A. Delahunt, the Reeveses' Providence lawyer; Winfield "Robbie" Reeves, Euchlin's brother; Robbie's son, Chester; T. B. Bryant, Euc's Washington and Lee classmate; my wife, Celeste; and me.

Ruth, an extremely large woman, was dressed neck to toe in stark white. Her stiffly starched uniform brushed against the walls on both sides of the narrow hallway as we followed. Her silent movement on gum-soled shoes gave the impression that she was gliding on air as she led us, single file, to the room where Mrs. Reeves had lived for nearly four years. In earlier days, it had been the dining room, but it now accommodated three residents. Two of the neatly made beds were empty, their occupants visible in wheelchairs through open French doors that led to the living room. Undistracted by us, they stared at a black-and-white television set, hypnotized by the garbled picture that rolled continuously.

In the third bed lay Mrs. Reeves, her tiny, delicate frame propped nearly upright. With wispy white hair and short bangs, bright blue eyes and rose-powdered cheeks and nose, she seemed at first to be ageless: a porcelain doll. She had reached that stage in life when, in appearance, she could grow no older. She was dressed in a pale pink flannel gown; her left arm rested on a decorated tissue box. On her wrist was a delicate silver-chain bracelet, its only charm a small replica of the Eiffel Tower. Paralyzed on her right side by a stroke suffered several years earlier, she was unable to move without assistance. The nurse brushed away the tears from her cheeks as she began to weep softly. After being introduced, she asked Celeste to take the room's lone chair, situated next to her bed.

"Why did Boy have to go first?" she asked aloud several times. Sobbing now, she added, "My hope was to have ten years with him. We were married for twenty-five."

Who was Boy? She must mean Mr. Reeves, but I did not inquire.

Looking at me, she said, "He told me of your visits. I am sorry I was not at home to greet you. He loved Washington and Lee."

We spoke little, beyond offering our condolences. Ruth, her size even more pronounced as she leaned over the tiny figure, tried to comfort Louise. The sorrow of her loss filled the room. We all felt awkward in our inability to console her.

A telephone call from Donald Delahunt three days earlier had informed me that Euchlin Reeves, hospitalized, had suffered a stroke, was paralyzed and unconscious. Later that same day came word that he had died. Mrs. Reeves had been informed and was grief-stricken. The same evening Delahunt telephoned to say that Mrs. Reeves was planning the funeral for the 13th and had requested that Celeste and I attend. He added that a wake would be held the evening before.

After flying from Washington to Boston, we drove a rented car directly to 89 Benevolent Street in Providence. It was the home where I had first met Euchlin Reeves three years earlier, in February, 1964.

The small house seemed to be exactly as it had been on my first visit. But was it? Without Mr. Reeves it would be a dormant storage shell, crammed with hundreds of lifeless objects. Hard-packed ice and snow led from the curbing to the front entrance, flush with the sidewalk. The Christmas wreath was made of spruce, dry and brown with a faded red ribbon. Was it the one that had been hanging there when I first knocked on the door three years earlier? It was possible. The symbol brought to mind my first meeting at 89 Benevolent Street.

This odyssey began in the autumn of 1963 with the arrival at Washington and Lee of a penny postcard bearing a Providence cancellation and a scene of the majestic dome of the white-marbled statehouse. The message was simple and direct: "Someday I may wish to make a donation of a work of art to the university. Are you interested?" It was signed, "Euc Reeves, '27 Law."

The postcard passed through a number of hands, including my own, without reaching anyone who had any real knowledge or interest in art. Reading the short text a second time, I paused on the words "donation" and "art."

A POSTCARD PURSUED

Remembering "Euchie" Reeves as a student of the Roaring Twenties, two very senior university officials questioned what good could possibly come from my pursuit. While respectful of their opinions, I was not deterred by their memories, now thirty years old. I volunteered to contact Mr. Reeves.

Two months had passed since the postcard arrived in Lexington, and it seemed prudent to telephone rather than write — first to explain the delay (I don't recall the excuse I offered), and then to determine, if possible, the true meaning of the postcard's message.

After only one ring, a gentle Southern accent answered. I introduced myself and made a veiled reference to his correspondence. Mr. Reeves seemed pleased to hear from someone connected with the university. Immediately inquiring of classmates, he spoke of the 1920s as though I had been a member of his class. I was a sympathetic listener and responded as though I, too, remembered those "good old days." As the conversation ended, we made arrangements to meet in Providence on my next trip to New York, in early February. Mr. Reeves urged me to arrive in time for lunch. Our talk had been pleasant and I looked forward to meeting this alumnus of another era. Neither of us mentioned "a donation of a work of art."

I arrived in New York on February 5, 1964, and checked into the Biltmore Hotel on East 43rd Street. Inquiring into train schedules from nearby Grand Central Terminal to Providence, I learned that my destination was a bit farther than the Connecticut suburbs I had initially assumed. Leaving New York very early on a Thursday morning, I met the incoming traffic of commuters that brings Grand Central to life each morning of the workweek. Breakfast in the train's dining car was pleasant and leisurely with ample time to anticipate the scheduled meeting.

Reaching the Providence train depot about 11 a.m., I found the city covered by an accumulation of several inches of ice and snow from recent storms. I hailed a taxi and the driver, accustomed to slippery streets, proceeded without mishap to College Hill, passing the Rhode Island School of Design and Brown University. I was entering a different world, as architecture of the eighteenth and nineteenth centuries surrounded me. It was a city frozen in time, both literally and figuratively. There were Georgian- and Federal-period houses, some two stories and others three, with Palladian windows and pilasters rising from ground to roof. Ornamental eagles and beautifully carved classic urns capped the columns of the houses along Benefit, Waterman and Power Streets. The great mansions we passed, one after another, gave me a preconception of the house I was about to enter.

"Donation" and "art" kept flashing through my mind. Did Mr. Reeves have a portrait by Charles Willson Peale, or one by Gilbert Stuart, a Rhode Island native, or perhaps one by John Singleton Copley of nearby Boston? After all, the homes we were passing must surely contain the finest examples of early Americana. A frightening thought occurred to me: Would I be able to converse with Mr. Reeves with any semblance of understanding?

The taxi turned onto Benevolent Street and stopped at the second house from the corner. I wondered aloud why the sudden halt. Surely this modest place could not be the Reeveses' home. But we were on Benevolent, and "89" was clearly marked. I protested, but the driver assured me there was no North or South Benevolent, no East or West Benevolent. "This is the only Benevolent Street in Providence," he said.

I paid the fare but requested the driver wait with the motor running while I made certain we had the correct address. The house, abutting the sidewalk, one room wide, and two and a half stories high, was covered with unpainted, weathered wooden shingles. No way, I thought, could this house contain any work of art.

My faint, hesitant rap of the metal doorknocker in the center of a Christmas wreath brought an answer from inside. "I'm coming," the accent was foreign. In the background I could hear a small dog barking, growing louder as he reached the entry. The door opened to reveal a stocky man in his forties, with black hair and very dark eyes. Was this the Mr. Reeves I had spoken with earlier?

Before either of us could speak, a voice inside the foyer said, "Is that you, Jim Whitehead? I hope you have come to stay two weeks. Joe has readied the guest room and bath." It was as though I was being welcomed from the columned piazza of a Southern plantation house. "Two weeks?" I thought. "I don't think this will last two minutes." I let my lifeline go, signaling the cab to leave. Had the university doubters been right about "Euchie"?

It was several moments before my eyes adjusted from the sun's bright glare on the white snow to the dark interior I had entered. The foyer was only three feet wide and four feet long. In that tight space, in addition to a small table against the right wall, I was one of three grown men and a barking dog. Mr. Reeves, sixty years old, immaculately groomed in a brown pinstriped suit, starched white shirt and silk tie with a diamond stick pin, grasped my hand with a hearty shake and introduced Joe Lombardi, the handyman who had answered the door. Jumping vertically was Hossy, the Reeves' toy Boston bull terrier. The welcome was complete. Joe and Hossy disappeared into the rear of the house, and Mr. Reeves, seemingly out of context and place, guided me slowly into the living room.

He cleared magazines, books and unopened mail from a faded upholstered chair of some age so I might sit. Over time, weight and wear had caused the webbing to disintegrate. I

89 Benevolent Street, Providence, 1964

cautiously lowered myself into the chair, feeling I was no more than four or five inches from the floor. As my eyes adjusted to the change in light, I slowly became aware of my surroundings. The room was about ten by twelve feet with a seven-foot ceiling. A double window faced the street where I had entered, and there was another large window on the outside wall. The room, wrapped in faded, water-stained wallpaper, contained a daybed, chest of drawers, secretary bookcase, slant-top desk, two chairs and a threadbare Oriental carpet. Draperies covered the windows, and on the walls were a pair of sconces, a mirror above the chest and several small paintings. Added to the overcrowded room was a small grand piano of ancient vintage, long silenced, with its keyboard flush against the wall at the front of the house.

Every flat surface I could see was covered with cups, saucers, plates, bowls, vases, pitchers, urns, auction catalogues and antiques journals. The only light came from a low-watt electric bulb, shadeless and hanging by a cord from the ceiling, a table lamp converted from oil to electricity, and a wrought iron standing lamp. A telephone in its cradle and a black-and-white television set, atop the piano — used only to watch the news, I was told — were the only evidence of the twentieth century.

Quickly glancing around the room, it became obvious that Mr. Reeves had carefully guided me along a three-foot aisle to my chair. Not only were the furniture surfaces covered with ceramics; items were stored under the bed, on and under the piano, atop and below the chairs. The drawers of the chest, the secretary bookcase, and the desk were overflowing with pieces of porcelain.

Mr. Reeves apologized that his wife was unable to greet me and explained she had not been well and was currently in a nursing home. "I expect her return within a few days," he explained. A hospital bed, readied with linens in the adjoining dining room, gave witness to his statement. That room was smaller than the one in which we sat, only about nine feet square. In addition to the hospital bed next to a large Victorian sideboard, there was a round pedestal dining table with four matching wooden chairs as well as a late-Empire-style sofa. On the wall above the sideboard was an oil painting of a hunter's trophy duck. Several smaller paintings covered the remaining wall space. Except for opened boxes of breakfast cereal, assorted small plastic containers of medicine, and a few pieces of unpolished silver on the dining table, all surfaces, including the hospital bed, were covered with dishes.

A narrow staircase, identical to another leading steeply from the foyer to the second floor, took space from the small room. The clutter of assorted objects on every step made it perilous to ascend or descend. A passing thought came to mind: If Joe had readied the guest room and bath on the second floor, how could I possibly reach them? But there was no reason to dwell on that question.

Sitting on the edge of his single bed with only a narrow aisle separating us, Mr. Reeves' story began to unfold. His memories of Washington and Lee were interspersed with his undergraduate days at Piedmont Academy in northern Georgia and at Emory University in Atlanta. He expressed pride in his Pi Kappa Phi fraternity membership and in college organizations at Washington and Lee devoted to drama (the Troubadour Theatre) and to music (the Glee Club and musical revues). Not surprisingly, his recollections of the university's quadrennial mock presidential nominating convention did not include a number of pranks still vivid in the minds of the college administrators. Eventually our conversation shifted from the campus in Lexington to life in Providence. It was not until later that I learned how an earlier profession brought him north.

Mr. Reeves made the point, several times, that his wife, Louise Herreshoff, was a great-great granddaughter of John Brown. Incorrectly, I assumed he was alluding to the abolitionist of Civil War notoriety. I soon learned that Mrs. Reeves' ancestor was of the eighteenth century and one of the most influential business leaders in New England.

The conversation turned to objects that surrounded us and how and where he and Mrs. Reeves acquired them over the years. The language of a scholar and a historian began to emerge. I was deeply impressed by the knowledge he possessed and attempted to cover my ignorance by responding with a nod or an "Oh, yes." He opened several books that were on his bed, pointing to pictures or descriptions of objects he and his wife owned. The words could have been from a foreign language and were impossible for me to translate. I was astounded at the value he ascribed to various pieces. "How could they possibly afford such extravagant objects and live in the surroundings visible to me?" I wondered, almost aloud. "How could a plate or a cup and saucer cost several hundred dollars and others even a thousand or more?"

Our meeting in the little room lasted less than an hour. I had not removed my overcoat for fear of sending whole boxes crashing to the floor. Too, an outmoded furnace provided only minimal heat throughout the first floor rooms. Shortly before noontime came the most welcome words of the morning. "I have made luncheon reservations at Carr's Tea Room. You will like it," Mr. Reeves said. The thought of a midday meal was less important than the prospect of warmer and brighter surroundings.

As we walked to the front door, I noticed a clear, plastic dry cleaner's bag hanging on the wall next to the foyer table. The plastic cover carried the message "Merry Christmas" printed in green and red letters. Inside the bag was a lady's gray silk dress. Strange, I thought, but made no comment. Standing at curbside, Joe opened the rear door to a black 1962 Cadillac Fleetwood. Other than Mr. Reeves' diamond stickpin, the car was the only sign of personal affluence I had seen. I

EUCHLIN REEVES WITH PORCELAIN FROM
THE REEVES COLLECTION, 93 BENEVOLENT STREET, PROVIDENCE

entered the car and sat on the comfortable back seat next to Mr. Reeves; Joe placed a wool lap robe over our knees. "Anita Hinckley, a close friend, will be joining us," Mr. Reeves said.

Within minutes Joe turned the car into a narrow alley and then into the backyard of one of the great 18th-century houses that I had passed earlier on Waterman Street. Mrs. Frank Hinckley, about eighty, tall and erect, was waiting at the rear entrance of her home. The door, I learned, led to a ballroom added to the mansion in the early part of the century for birthday parties, dances and receptions. Dressed entirely in black, wearing a cape that swept the ground and a large hat, she maneuvered well with a cane and Joe's steady arm as he assisted her to the limousine.

How could the car be extracted from the tight quarters of the small driveway, I wondered silently. I soon found out: the Cadillac, motor idle, turned 180 degrees. Joe had pushed the car from the outside on a mechanical turntable, installed for use in an earlier century to accommodate horse-drawn carriages.

After being introduced, Mrs. Hinckley expressed her regret that "dear Louise," a lifelong friend, was unable to be with us. She talked of her visit to Washington and Lee when she chaperoned her daughter at a Fancy Dress Ball, recalling her stay at the Dutch Inn, visiting the historic chapel on the campus in which Robert E. Lee, his forebears and his descendants were buried, and having a delightful time. Mr. Reeves glowed with pride as she talked about his alma mater. Mrs. Hinckley, a professional writer by interest and talent, devoted her skills to tales of her favorite subjects, Rhode Island and Narragansett Bay.

Carr's Tea Room, situated in an imposing two-story dark-red brick house near the campus of Brown University, catered to faculty members and businessmen who found it convenient for light lunches and special dinners. Once seated, with our orders placed for chicken salad, tomato aspic and Parker House rolls, the conversation between Mrs. Hinckley and Mr. Reeves centered mainly on their collections of porcelain.

"Have you found the pair of Wedgwood candle sticks with lemon-drop crystals?" she asked Mr. Reeves. "Louise was so anxious to add them to the Washington bust with the Adams base."

"What in the hell is she talking about?" I thought. He in turn inquired if she had located a Chinese Rose Medallion helmet creamer to match her nineteenth-century tea service. It was clear I could add little to the conversation. I was hearing the language, the excitement and enthusiasm of true collectors. They paid little attention to the meal of lady-size portions or to my request to have the breadbasket replenished.

As we left Carr's, Mr. Reeves accepted Mrs. Hinckley's invitation for a "stop by" visit to her home. It would give me the opportunity of viewing the interior of an architectural gem and experiencing again the marvel of the unusual turntable.

The Hinckley home, a national treasure, was a wooden wonder. Three stories high, the outside ornamentation gave the appearance of a highly decorated wedding cake with fluted pilasters, stone groins and twenty carved classic urns spaced at intervals along the balustrade on the second and third levels. A thirty-seven-paned Palladian window on the second-floor front was the centerpiece of design. The interior brick chimneys on each side of the house extended from the basement and became exposed only once they reached the third floor. The interior millwork was no less dramatic as it showcased the furniture, art and memorabilia collected by the family over the better part of two centuries. The Rose Medallion tea set discussed at lunch became the focal point of our brief tour.

"Please give my love to dear Louise," Mrs. Hinckley called out as we departed and the car moved gently on the turntable.

Mr. Reeves confided that Rose Medallion was not his favorite Chinese porcelain, but his wife loved its varied decorations and especially the vivid gem-like colors. The statement, a casual comment and barely audible, was without meaning to me. My mind was on what I hoped by that point would be our next destination: the Providence railroad station.

I was wrong. Mr. Reeves politely asked Joe to drive to the John Brown House at the corner of Power and Benefit Streets. He reminded me again that his wife was the great-great granddaughter of the house's original owner. The first view from the car of the eighteenth-century house explained in part the emphasis placed on Mrs. Reeves' ancestry. Grand in scale and setting, the three-story mansion of red brick and white trim had been in recent times the headquarters of the Rhode Island Historical Society. Proceeding past tall gateposts, with mounted marble busts of Summer and Winter said to have been acquired from Versailles by Brown after the French Revolution, we were greeted warmly by the resident director of the Society and his wife, Clifford and Eleanor Monahon.

Mr. Reeves was in his element, pointing with theatrical gestures to various items that belonged to his wife and him. They had lent the society numerous porcelain pieces for an exhibit of Rhode Island decorative arts dating from about 1730 to 1810. (What, I thought, from the house at 89 Benevolent that I had seen in the morning could possibly qualify for inclusion in the exhibition?)

As we toured the rooms and saw the parlor where Mrs. Reeves' great grandmother, Sarah Brown, was married in 1801 to Karl Frederich Herreshoff, it became clear why John Quincy Adams had described the house as the "most magnificent and elegant private mansion I have ever seen on this continent."

Area walls were originally covered with colorful paper from France, and later scenes depicted George Washington's first inauguration. Paintings by Robert Feke and Gilbert Stuart,

THE JOHN BROWN HOUSE, PROVIDENCE

NOW THE HEADQUARTERS OF THE RHODE ISLAND HISTORICAL SOCIETY

artists of the 1700s, were among the works that adorned the walls. Furniture by Newport cabinet craftsmen John Townsend and John Goddard were in evidence, and I first heard of delicate porcelains brought from Canton, China, on Brown's ship *General Washington,* inaugurating Rhode Island's trade with the Orient in 1787.

Descending from a second floor sitting room, where tea had been served, to the entrance hall below, holding firmly to the polished mahogany handrail of the grand staircase, we left behind nearly 200 years of history.

After goodbyes to our hosts, we headed toward the exit from the grounds at the gateposts. Mr. Reeves, as though an eigthteenth-century visitor of John Brown, murmured, "President George Washington was a guest here, you know." I nodded.

Joe drove us back to the Reeveses' home but stopped the car just beyond the door of 89 Benevolent in front of the house next door. The numerals "93" were barely visible on the front door. Mr. Reeves turned to me and asked, "Would you like to see our little museum?"

"Of course," I replied somewhat hesitantly, beginning my fourth adventure of the day.

A small garden of leafless trees and bushes, behind a waist-high iron fence, separated the two small dwellings at 89 and 93 Benevolent. Several outdoor metal chairs were anchored to a cement base by link chains. Deep snow piled high on each seat would remain their only occupant until spring.

The "little museum," a dark-red brick house two-and-a-half stories high, was a slightly larger mirror image of its next-door neighbor. Iron burglar bars were attached to the ground floor windows. Five or six safety locks secured the ornamental, metal-front door. Removing a chain heavy with keys from his overcoat pocket, Mr. Reeves began inserting the correct key into the proper lock. Knowing the direction to turn each key was essential. The Reeves had devised a combination system by using standard Yale locks that, when correctly turned, opened the old door.

We entered a crowded vestibule, pitch black dark, the temperature well below freezing. The interior of the house was without comfort, all utilities having been disconnected several years earlier. The wall to the left of the door, about five feet wide, was covered with an ornate, gold-framed mirror reaching from floor to ceiling. Only our shadowy surreal figures were visible through its blanket of dust. Mr. Reeves, pulling back the pair of worn draperies that covered the front window of the parlor, allowed cloudy daylight to filter in. Particles of dirt, long embedded in the fabric and now disturbed, fluttered throughout the room and settled on all surfaces.

The room was haphazardly filled with old furniture and ceramics. In contrast to 89, there was no aisle for passage; a step in any direction was nearly impossible. Flashlight in hand, Mr. Reeves pointed from one treasure to another. The exposure to fine decorative arts at Mrs. Hinckley's home and later at the John Brown House caused me to realize that, while ignorant of the origin or provenance of an object, treasures of another century surrounded me.

The furniture in 89, the home next door, was mainly Victorian. In 93, Euchlin Reeves aimed the light at chairs, tables and chests he described as Queen Anne, Chippendale and Hepplewhite. Some pieces, he said, had been made by New England craftsmen from Rhode Island and Massachusetts, others from New York and Philadelphia. Carefully stepping over and between the furniture and the porcelain spread on the floor, the light bounced from one object to another. As in 89, all surfaces were covered with porcelain, stacked one piece atop another on the floor, tables, chairs and settee.

In rapid fire, Mr. Reeves described items and dispensed information on the history of Chinese hard-paste porcelain.

Developed in the ninth century, the exotic treasures of Cathay became known to Europeans upon the return of Marco Polo from China in the thirteenth century. The secret formula for hard-paste porcelain, known for centuries only to the potters of the Orient, was accidentally discovered at Meissen in Germany in the early eighteenth century by the alchemist Johann Frederick Bottger under the patronage of Augustus the Strong. The combination of refined white clay known as "kaolin" and the mineral rock called "petunse," fired at high temperatures, resulted in the fragile, translucent porcelains, so cherished by seventeenth- and eighteenth-century royalty and nobility in Europe and Asia.

I did not understand or remember the extraordinary information Euchlin Reeves was sharing so freely. Looking, listening and stepping gingerly among the fragile collection, I comprehended only the slightest amount of the history that enveloped me.

Completely out of character, or so it seemed, was a colorful painting of an elderly woman hanging in the parlor. She wore a heart-shaped diamond brooch at the neckline of her dress. My eyes immediately focused on the subject's unusual and vivid features, with red ears and purple eyes. Another portrait of the woman, almost identical, hung in the adjoining dining room. I assumed they were paintings of Mrs. Reeves, as Joe had told me earlier in the day, in private and in a muted tone, "She is older than her husband." Surely the portraits were not the "work of art" he had mentioned when he first wrote to the university. I decided not to ask.

As we walked from the parlor to the adjoining dining room, Reeves' voice grew stronger and more expressive as he spotted an object that took him back in memory to years past. He delighted in displaying his knowledge as he shuffled items of porcelain, silver and furniture. Some of the antiques were being moved for the first time in years.

THE "LITTLE MUSEUM,"
93 BENEVOLENT STREET, PROVIDENCE, 1964

Standing in the center of a vast collection, Euchlin Reeves was giving life to inanimate objects lovingly assembled by a couple who found great satisfaction in the pursuit, acquisition and research of each treasure. Piece after piece, buried over time in a lifeless tomb — each had a history all its own.

As we neared the pantry, just beyond the dining room, I hoped our tour was at an end. The frigid and foreign surroundings had become nearly unbearable. But Mr. Reeves removed from the rear wall an oriental rice paper scroll depicting sacred birds with black and white feathers and a small patch of red plumage capping their heads. It seemed the flock in flight was attempting to escape. I wished I could follow them.

The delicate paper covered a steel door with a combination lock. "It has been closed for several years," he said. With the correct combination and determined strength, he slowly opened the door, which creaked in great pain. Behind the steel door was a pair of gray metal doors, and as they were opened, the air from the damp, cold, musty stone vault blew directly against our faces. For a moment it was impossible to breathe. Only after my host directed the beam of light into the black interior could I see the contents.

Just inside the dank vault, a wooden drop-leaf table buckled under the weight of stacks of porcelain. If so much as a plate or even a saucer were added to the accumulation, surely a hundred or more items would crash to the cement floor. Subdued light fell on one object after another, which Mr. Reeves described as once having belonged to patriots of early American history.

"That is the Chinese tea set that belonged to Paul Revere. Do you see his initial P. R.?"

Continuing he said, "Mrs. Reeves bought it from a distant cousin, Mrs. George Howarth, whose mother, Mrs. Sears, acquired it many years ago from an unmarried daughter of Revere … George Washington owned the plate over there.

"The service was ordered from Canton on the *Empress of China,* the first ship to sail out of New York harbor to the Orient from the new republic following the signing of the Treaty of Paris in 1783.

"General Robert E. Lee's father, Light Horse Harry Lee, helped Washington acquire the service when it arrived from Canton," Reeves went on enthusiastically. "Light Horse is buried in Lee Chapel."

I nodded vigorously, as it was, at last, a fact I did know.

"The decoration is Fame holding the insignia of the Society of the Cincinnati. Members were officers who served with Washington during the Revolutionary War," he explained.

The light fell on a large platter with Chinese decorations of a river scene and the Eight Immortals. Mr. Reeves noted that it had belonged to Governor DeWitt Clinton of New York. "His initials intertwine with those of his wife, Maria Franklin, and form the 'D M F C' cipher on the border," he said. "They were married in 1796."

"The soup bowl in the rear with the motto 'Spero,' which means 'Hope,' was owned by Elias Hasket Derby of Salem, Massachusetts," he went on. "Like John Brown, my wife's great-great grandfather, he was also in the China trade." The light continued to glide from one object to another.

He continued, "The large punch bowl has a rust-colored eagle on both sides with a sunburst in orange and gold. The bird is an adaptation by a Chinese artist of the bald eagle from the Great Seal of the United States.

"It was given to Kiliaen Van Rensselaer of New York by the United States Congress in recognition of his financial support during the American Revolution. You can see the initials 'K. V. R.' and the date, 1801, on the inside bottom of the bowl. Few pieces of Oriental porcelain made for the western market carry an underglaze date. We bought it from David Stockwell's shop near Wilmington, Delaware."

Mr. Reeves pointed the flashlight to a large, highly decorated bowl that appeared very much like one I had seen at the John Brown House.

"There's our Hong Bowl!" he exclaimed. "Just like the one owned by Norman Herreshoff, my wife's nephew, that we saw this afternoon. Do you see the American flag?"

I couldn't. "The decoration shows the warehouses along the Pearl River in Canton where foreigners traded with the Chinese. We were offered $25,000 for ours. I understand there are only six extant from the same period with our country's flag."

Covered with years of dust was a large octagonal platter with delicate handles. "The Meissen platter," he explained, "was bought by my wife when she lived in Europe. It was modeled and decorated by the artisan Johann Kandler in the early eighteenth century and is from the swan service made for Count DeBruhl of Dresden. Very rare!" I had no reason to think otherwise.

Attempting to concentrate on his every word and show interest in the vivid descriptions, while shivering from the freezing chill, I ceased thinking of porcelain and weather when Mr. Reeves handed me the flashlight and invited me to step into the vault. I politely declined. After all, I was in a strange house with a man I had met only that day and surely the steel doors could be slammed easily — and *that* would teach me never to pursue a "work of art" again.

I did place one foot inside the dark interior, however, keeping the other squarely anchored to the pantry floor and my free hand firmly attached to the door's handle. The half-way measure was brief. A second morbid thought occurred: did the section of the vault behind the second set of doors contain something other than porcelain? It was best I leave that question to myself.

A FRAGILE UNION

Rapidly retreating, I passed the light back to the owner as the batteries began to fail and February darkness soon consumed the limited illumination throughout the house.

Euchlin Reeves had moved into the brick house following his marriage to Louise Herreshoff Eaton. As their insatiable drive for additional acquisitions seldom dimmed and their collection grew and grew, it became necessary to buy the little frame house next door at 89 Benevolent where we had met earlier in the day. Their former residence was rarely entered except when additional purchases were made; each would be placed atop an older item, rarely to be moved again. The highly personal collection that began as an orderly display of antiques for their pleasure and viewing by friends and other collectors slowly became unmanageable. Dust had settled for fifteen years on every surface, covering in some cases the designs on the porcelain, the grain of the woods of the furniture and the patterns of the fabrics.

As we prepared to leave, I could only imagine what the second floor was like and certainly had not the slightest idea of the contents of the attic beyond. Drawing the draperies together over the front window and closing and securing the front door, lock by lock, we left 93 and the "little museum." The iron fence steadied our walk on the icy path to 89 as my mind raced from one bizarre thought to another of the incredible day.

The small frame house felt much warmer than it had been when I arrived earlier in the day. The lamps and the hanging bulb added a pleasant glow. Hossy, the black-and-white terrier, was quieter and seldom left Mr. Reeves' side. After having breathed dust and stale air for two hours, I welcomed his offer of a drink — a glass of Manhattan cocktail mix. He cleared space on the crowded dining room table, asked me to be seated, then placed two clear jelly glasses on the bare surface and poured the syrupy liquid with great finesse. Placing on the table two dime-store blue-and-white Willow Ware plates, he announced that "faithful Joe" had prepared us a supper before leaving earlier in the afternoon.

Dinner consisted of thin slices of salt- and smoke-cured country ham remaining from a Christmas gift by South Carolina relatives, baked biscuits and canned pork and beans. It was delicious and ample. I chuckled to myself at the irony of being surrounded in every direction by treasures of priceless porcelain, silver and crystal, yet dining in such a modest fashion.

The meal was not important, however. It was what Euchlin Reeves said during supper that mattered most.

"If the university is interested, I will bring the major share of the collection to Lexington after Mrs. Reeves' death, provided there is a facility to house it."

He then added, "At my death the collection will go to the university as a memorial to my wife. This cannot be done until after Dol dies."

Now I knew the identity of Dol, as he used the name earlier in the day. It was the contraction for the southern term of endearment "darling." Indicating a deep interest in his thoughtful and generous proposal, I agreed to present it to the university president upon my return to the campus.

As we stood in the tiny vestibule waiting for the taxi to return me to the railroad station, Mr. Reeves pointed to the plastic bag I had noticed on arriving. As though contemplating an unhappy event, he said, "Dol will be buried in that dress."

◆

Three years later, I stood beside Mrs. Reeves' bed in Ruth's Nursing Home as she mourned the death of Boy. It was her husband — not she — whose funeral would be held the next day.

CHAPTER

8

THE WAKE

"The wake for Mr. Reeves is scheduled for eight o'clock this evening at D. W. Bellows & Son Funeral Home in Pawtucket," the family lawyer said as we left the nursing home.

Then, as though it were an afterthought, he added, "Mr. Reeves' last will and testament did not include Washington and Lee University."

The statement's meaning was as powerful a shock as being in the epicenter of a violent earthquake. The after-tremors came when he noted, "Mr. Reeves never mentioned his plans for the collection to Mrs. Reeves. He was fearful she would want it given to Brown, the university named for her ancestors." It became clear why it never seemed convenient for me to meet his wife.

The years spent developing this gift — the "work of art" — had come to naught. Fred Cole, Washington and Lee's president, had encouraged me to pursue the collection for the university, but, now, it was apparent that the nay-sayers had been right all along.

Three years had passed since I returned from my first visit with Mr. Reeves. I had spent the trip from Providence back to New York that evening filling a legal pad with notes and descriptions, many of the words spelled phonetically, of my day at 89 and 93 Benevolent Street.

Before attending the wake still in a state of semi-shock after hearing the crushing news only a few hours earlier, Celeste and I were having an early evening dinner with Caroline Cole, daughter of President Cole. She was on the administrative staff of Brown University's Pembroke College. My chair at dinner, though occupied, could have as well been empty. Thoughts were elsewhere. Caroline with her Washington and Lee connection had become acquainted with Mr. Reeves and members of the family over the same period of time that I came to know and respect Mr. Reeves, and she, too, had been invited to the wake.

Darkness and sub-zero weather complicated our efforts to find the funeral home on the outskirts of Providence, at 85 Park Place in Pawtucket. Fortunately a large electric sign reading "Bellows" became visible through the darkness. We arrived at exactly eight o'clock.

The funeral establishment, in past years a private residence, had enlarged front doors to accommodate the purpose it now served. Two soft-voiced undertakers greeted us in the hallway just inside the entry and ushered us into a combination parlor and viewing room. We faced directly at Mr. Reeves' open casket just six feet away. To our right lay five rows of four folding chairs. Mistaken for family members, we were seated on the front row, just three feet from the casket. Eight mourners sat behind us. At first, I avoided looking directly at Mr. Reeves' body; but it soon became impossible to avoid the sight.

Long-stemmed crimson roses, cascading down on all sides, draped the closed end of the gray metal casket. Sprays of carnations, gladiolus and chrysanthemums banked each end.

No whispers or music. Was the wake over or had it begun? The answer was soon apparent as a clang of metal striking metal and the rumbling of shuffling feet in the hallway broke the eerie silence. Our eyes shifted immediately to the open door on our left. To our astonishment and disbelief, Mrs. Reeves, sitting in a wheelchair, was rolled into the room. Dressed in a black wool coat, a matching cap with a tiny black bow on the bill, her legs covered with the Fleetwood's lap robe, this small, fragile woman, confined to a nursing-home bed for four years, braved one of the winter's coldest nights to attend her husband's wake.

Reaching the side of the casket, she said," I can't see him, I can't see him."

The attendants, assisted by Chester Reeves, her husband's nephew, lifted the chair and she extended her left arm to touch her husband's brow. She sobbed, and the mourners wept. After a seemingly interminable length of time, she withdrew her hand and the chair was lowered and wheeled backward. Never once changing the direction of her stare, she was unaware or unconcerned with others in the room. The wake was over.

The Reeves family from South Carolina asked us to join the cortege to Mount Auburn Cemetery in Cambridge the next morning. We accepted. Boston's Logan Airport, our departure point, was nearby.

My thoughts, after returning from the wake to the Sheraton-Biltmore Hotel, were of the years I had spent in coming to know Euchlin Reeves — a professional and personal relationship developed by letters, long-distance telephone conversations and occasional visits to Providence. He honored me after a year or so by asking for advice on certain purchases he had in mind. My usual reply, given unhesitatingly, suggested that he offer an amount less than the dealer was asking. When it worked, he gave undue credit for my knowledge.

Unable to sleep after a tumultuous day, I leafed through a blue-leather three-ring binder, placed in my briefcase while packing for the funeral trip to Providence. In addition to pictures of the university campus the binder contained the floor plan of Col Alto, the proposed site for the collection, along with interior pictures of its vacant rooms. Col Alto, a red-brick Georgian mansion with twenty rooms surrounded by seven acres of lawn, formal boxwood gardens and century-old maple trees, had been bequeathed to the university a few years earlier, and its stateliness made it an ideal showcase for the porcelain treasures.

Also in the binder were notes from Mr. Reeves regarding the gift and, more important, his words, "The Collection, when I die will be given to Washington and Lee in honor of my wife, Louise Herreshoff Reeves."

If Mr. Reeves did not include the university in his will, was it possible that his brother, Robbie Reeves, and his lawyer, Donald Delahunt, knew of his wishes? Robbie, in his late seventies, who had visited and cared for Euchlin when he was ill, was the oldest of three brothers and long retired. Brother Chester, an authority and dealer in antiques, had died in the 1950s.

Robbie and I had met on one of my Providence trips. He would spend time in Providence when Euchlin suffered a series of "pin strokes" as the doctors described them. A visiting nurse, Beulah Anderson, assisted as best she could. Fannie, Robbie's wife, was a lovely southern lady several years younger than her husband. She was a schoolteacher in Charleston and not always able to accompany Robbie to Providence. She managed to provide moral strength, however, when it was most needed.

Robbie visited Dol, his sister-in-law, each day at Ruth's Nursing Home during his brother's illness. Dol and Boy had never been parted during their married life until a stroke left her bedridden. Boy's attempt to move with her to Ruth's was unsuccessful. Euchlin gave Robbie $2 each day for carfare to and from visits with Dol, for laundry and other necessities. No matter the season, Robbie wore a wool suit with starched shirt and conservative tie. Outside, he donned a felt or straw hat, cocked to one side.

Robbie never felt at home in Providence and traveled there from South Carolina only if the signs of the Zodiac were correctly aligned. He was constantly distressed at the cluttered condition of 89 Benevolent and often would say, "Our mother would turn over in her grave if she knew how Euchie was living." But Euchlin was oblivious to his surroundings. Caring for Dol and researching and adding items to their collection consumed his time. Creature comforts were not a priority.

Studying the architectural drawings, Mr. Reeves had found great pleasure in mentally placing the rare and beautiful items in Col Alto's various rooms, as he recalled how he and his wife had planned their "little museum." It was a pastime that would occupy most of his day when not visiting Dol at the nursing home.

His letters to me were exacting in detail:

> Our gold leaf metal eagle with a wing span of three feet will be placed over the front door, it will set the tone for the entrance hall where items belonging to presidents of the United States will be placed in cases along each wall. The Chinese export porcelain dinner plate that belonged to George Washington, dating to about 1786, showing winged Fame holding the insignia of the Order of the Cincinnati, will have the place of honor just inside the door. Light Horse Harry Lee, who along with his son General Robert E. Lee, is buried in Lee Chapel helped Washington acquire the service. Other Washington items, a Chinese export tea cup in sepia color depicting Washington's tomb, his name and a weeping willow tree in the background will be placed in the parlor to the left. The garniture vase with the scene of Mount Vernon will be centered on the parlor's mantle beneath the reverse paintings on glass of George and his wife Martha. Three Chippendale style chairs, attributed to the furniture craftsman Gillingham, were once owned by Washington during his presidency in Philadelphia.

They descended in the Custis family. We bought them from David Stockwell's shop near Wilmington, Delaware. They will be placed by the large tilttop tea table from Connecticut, on which by tradition Washington and Rochambeau planned the siege of Yorktown. We acquired it at auction.

The parlor will be predominately items of porcelain made at Chingtechen, China and decorated by special order for the American market between 1785 and 1810 at the port of Canton. There will be punch bowls, chargers, platters, cups, saucers, plates, cider flagons, coffee and teapots. Most will have Spartan decorations with the American flag, ships flying the Stars and Stripes, the American bald eagle and the Great Seal of the United States.

If room permits I would like to have the Paul Revere service in the same room. It has his initials "PR" in gold, with a border decoration in green and purple with the grape and leaf pattern. The papers and provenance are in our lockbox. [Paul Revere's will does not mention a Chinese tea set, but the inventory of his house at the time of his death in 1818 lists two.]

In the American room I have decided to display the blue, white and gold bordered plate of Archibald Bulloch of Georgia. He was an ancestor of Theodore Roosevelt. Also, the soup plate of Elias Hasket Derby of Salem, Massachusetts. He, along with Dol's great-great grandfather John Brown, were very early tradesmen with the Chinese after 1783. We have a very fine example of the Great Seal on two double-handled cups that belonged to Dol's great-great uncle Moses Brown. There will be the Arms of Liberty bowl, with portraits of John Wilkes and the English Judge Mansfield. Wilkes, a member of Parliament, advocated the independence of the American colonies.

On second thought, although it was made for the Lee family in Coton, England in the 1730s, I feel the large charger should hang next to the George Washington plate in the center hall. The artwork is superb with the smallest detail on the border showing the Port of London, the London Bridge, the dome of St. Paul's Cathedral and the scene of Canton, along the Pearl River in China. In the center is the Lee coat-of-arms with the squirrel as the family crest."

On paper he furnished room after room. He mentally transported himself from his tiny living quarters in Providence to the grand and spacious mansion in Lexington. The second parlor, formerly the music room, would showcase Chippendale and hand-painted Sheraton furniture, with Chinese porcelains made for the English and Continental market showing religious and mythological scenes with decorations in encre de chine (India black ink), special-order services with the coats of arms for the nobility, items depicting scenes of the Chinese at work and play, the evolution of the color pink on Chinese ceramics after the 1720s. Famille Noir (decoration with black), Famille Verte (decoration with green) and Famille Rose (decoration with pink) would be exhibited if space permitted; otherwise the beautiful pieces would be placed in the side entrance hall just before the grand dining room.

No detail was missed:

> We will place plate shelves on all the walls and on the ceiling with special tracks for the Rose Medallion, Rose Canton and Rose Mandarin. The banquet table will have place settings of seven for twenty-four guests. The jewel tones of pink, green, yellow, black, white and gold will sparkle under the crystal chandelier that I will be buying for the room. Dol loves the vibrant colors. Most pieces in the room will date to the 19th century. The winding stair case wall will be lined with Japanese and Chinese Imari plates, with vivid blue and iron red flowers.

There would be a room of eighteenth-century English ceramics, including items of Worcester from the Dr. John Wall period of mid-eighteenth century. Wedgwood, Staffordshire, Caughley, Coalport, Derby, Lowestoft, Bow, Newhall and Chelsea. Creamware (Queensware), pearlware, salt glaze, and soft- and hard-paste porcelain would highlight the English room:

> Period furniture will complement the ceramics. The mantle garniture will be the three piece Wedgwood candleholders with clear and lemon color crystal drops, and pale blue neoclassical bases. They will flank a matching centerpiece with a white ceramic bust of George Washington dressed in a Roman toga. Liverpool jugs with patriotic scenes of transfer decorations will line the shelf below the crown molding.

Later, I would discover that the jugs contained affectionate notes from Boy to Dol and dried petals of crimson roses he had given her on their anniversaries and her birthdays.

His explicit instructions continued:

> The large white porcelain tray that I have told you about with applied rope shaped handles and flowers made at Meissen in the 1730s for Count de Bruhl and decorated by Johann Kandler that was bought by Dol in Germany years ago, will serve as the centerpiece of the German and Austrian 18th-century collection. . . .
>
> French porcelain with early Sevres marks should be displayed with Chantilly, Rouen and ceramics from Limoges.
>
> I want the paint for the walls and ceilings in each room to be the dominant base color of the porcelain; white with a tint of gray in the Chinese export rooms, cream color for the English room, stark white in the German room and mauve for the French room.

Mr. Reeves would change his mind from time to time about the arrangements for exhibit, but the project appeared to shed years from his age and add a new spirit to his lonely life without Dol. I learned they had never been apart for one night until her illness required attention she could not receive at home.

Our iron garden furniture will be just right in the box wood circle as you approach Col Alto. My brother Robbie and his wife Fannie will live with me on the second floor. We will act as guides and charge a fee, say five dollars. The money will go to the University.

I wondered if he had ever mentioned his dream to Robbie and Fannie.

During the project of creating on paper an exhibition center, I was being exposed to a period of history that had found little place in my professional world of finance. In the evenings, I began to study ceramics and eighteenth-century American history, from the resource materials, books, catalogues and periodicals that Mr. Reeves supplied or suggested. Travels for the university to different parts of the country presented opportunities to seek out museums and galleries that housed antique porcelains and furniture. Mr. Reeves became the teacher and I his willing student, all the while attempting to convey the significance of the collection to my associates at the university.

Some understood. Most did not.

CHAPTER

9

THE FUNERAL

Friday the 13th of January, 1967, the day of Euchlin Reeves' funeral, was cold and overcast with snow predicted. The drive to Boston from Providence as part of a funeral procession was not an appealing thought.

Arriving at Bellows Funeral Home, Celeste and I were directed in our rental car to the second space behind the hearse. Again, we were mistaken for family members; Fannie and son Chester and T. B. Bryant were in the funeral home limousine behind us. The space directly in front of us was vacant but only for a few minutes. As though on cue the Reeves' black Cadillac arrived.

Delahunt, the lawyer, was driving with Robbie at his side. In the rear sat Dol, so small and fragile, dressed in the black coat and cap she had worn the night before. Propped up with large white pillows, leaning against Ruth, the nursing home proprietress, Dol was barely visible. Against prudent reasoning, she would make the four-hour round-trip drive to Mount Auburn Cemetery in Cambridge. Twice within less than twenty-four hours, she had braved frigid weather, icy roads and threatening snow to mourn her husband. She personally laid out each detail of the funeral arrangements.

Entering Mount Auburn, the hearse proceeded to Willow Avenue, past hundreds of tombstones, monuments and vaults, each capped with snow. The procession of four vehicles came to a halt near a tall twenty-foot gray stone obelisk with the name "JOHN DYER" clearly visible on its base. Just below the name was etched "The Righteous Shall Be In Everlasting Remembrance." The monument stood on a high rise of ground. Three wide stone steps led to the base. On the left side of the steps was a granite marker etched with "LOUISE HERRESHOFF REEVES." It looked as though it had been carved recently. To the right of the steps was the open grave, the mound of fresh dirt covered with snow. A matching granite marker for "EUCHLIN DALCHO REEVES" was in place.

The procession was met by the Reverend W. Owings Stone of Barrington, Rhode Island, rector of St. John's Episcopal Church, where Dol and Boy had eloped twenty-five years earlier. The brief funeral service was conducted near the open door of the Reeveses' car: The inclement weather forced Dol to remain inside. As the casket was taken from the warmth of the hearse, the snowflakes fell on the blanket of roses and began to melt. It seemed as though each rose joined Dol in weeping. We stood at the side of the open car throughout the service and heard her say, "I will be back. I will be back." After the final prayer, we said goodbye to Mrs. Reeves and the family. Despondently, I handed Robbie the blue leather binder I had brought from Lexington.

Was I mourning the loss of a friend — or the loss of a collection? In retrospect it was both.

◆

The return flight to Virginia provided time to construct an explanation for Mr. Reeves' omission of Washington and Lee from his will. The best and most honest statement for those who were confident of a successful conclusion to a three-year effort and to those who felt certain "nothing good would ever come from Euchie Reeves," would be to confine my remarks to the funeral and the extremely brave and gracious wife, Louise Herreshoff Reeves. It was a wise decision.

Within two days of returning to the campus, a telephone call from the Reeveses' lawyer brought news that he and Robbie shared with Dol the materials in the blue binder. Robbie explained to her that Euchie had wanted the collection to be given to Washington and Lee in her memory.

"No!" she had said emphatically, "That cannot be. I will give the collection to the university in my own will in memory of Boy's mother, Mrs. Chester Reeves, and my Aunt Lizzie."

The news thrilled and relieved me. No longer was it necessary to explain Euc Reeves' will. I had convinced myself that it was his honest intention to provide for the university, but he had delayed his inclination because of his poor health. Like the porcelain that surrounded him, he felt immortal.

My elation was short lived. The following morning, Delahunt called to inform me that Mrs. Reeves had changed her mind. "She is not leaving the collection to the university in her will," he said.

Then he added, "She wishes to give it now."

Her lawyer explained that Mrs. Reeves offered to give Robbie any of the collection he wanted, especially items that had descended in the Reeves family, and that the rest, except for a few Brown–Herreshoff family pieces, would go to Washington and Lee.

Dol's concern over the safety of the collection in the unattended houses at 89 and 93 brought about her determination to make decisions immediately. She gave her Cadillac to Robbie and Fannie, and through her will, she would bequeath to Robbie her stock portfolio, selections of furniture and ceramics, and her jewelry. She would designate that both properties be given to her late husband's family. Minor bequests went to her half-nephew, Norman Herreshoff, and her cousin, Louise Kilton DeWolf, both of Bristol.

Mrs. Reeves was anxious to transfer the collection as quickly as possible to Lexington. She was aware of student unrest on college campuses across the country and of the demonstrations against the Vietnam War at Brown University and the Rhode Island School of Design, both institutions a few blocks from 89 and 93. Though the collection was generally unknown to outsiders, vandals could have easily destroyed the contents of both houses.

Philip Budrose of Marblehead, Massachusetts, a member of the National Fine Arts Appraisers Association, was retained to evaluate the contents of the houses. Valuing each of the thousands of items was nearly impossible and would have taken months. He could only estimate as he moved from room to room, and would remark as he threaded the maze, "I will give $75,000 for what I see here, and $175,000 for the items there." So it went until he arrived at a valuation, which he passed on verbally to the lawyer. I was never told, and I never asked, the final tally.

Budrose visited Dol after the appraisal. "Your collection is the finest to come to light in the past twenty years," he told her. She was overjoyed and replied, "I wish my husband could hear you say that."

Arthur Lans of Lans Transfer Company, Providence, was contracted to begin the task of packing the collection. He estimated ten days for the job. It took nearly three months.

The thick stone walls of the vault and the brick of 93 maintained a near-freezing temperature for weeks after the outside snow and ice began to melt in late March of 1967. Utility service had been disconnected when the Reeveses moved next door, fifteen years earlier. Activating the outdated heating, electricity and water systems would have been extremely dangerous. Rewiring the house was out of the question. To proceed with the project, heavy-duty electric extension cords were run across the frozen garden from 89 to 93.

Using one portable electric heater in the living room, Arthur Lans kept his hands just warm enough to handle the ice-cold ceramics. An electric light bulb, surrounded by a protective metal cage, hung from an antique gas chandelier. Beneath the light and next to the heater was a table for wrapping and packing the objects in cartons and cardboard barrels.

To avoid extreme temperature changes, the porcelains were gradually moved from the vault, to the pantry, to the dining room and then to the living room for packing. That process alone took several weeks.

Euchlin's brother, Robbie, came from South Carolina to oversee the packing and to visit Dol in Ruth's Nursing Home. Daily, he would report to her the status of the packing. She would reminisce and say: "Boy liked objects belonging to historic American figures, and I love beautiful things."

When the packing job was completed in April of that year, I flew to Providence to sign the acceptance papers. The furniture and cartons and barrels of porcelain were being placed on the Allied Van when I arrived.

Robbie and I were standing on the sidewalk along the iron fence when Mr. Lans called to me from the attic window of 93. "There're some old frames up here, Mr. Whitehead. Do you want 'em?"

Fatefully, I called back, "If there's room in the van after the furniture and porcelains are packed, put them in." Our art students were always looking for frames for their annual spring show. Lans packed the frames in cardboard boxes and found room in the van.

The contents of 89 and 93 arrived in Lexington in mid-April 1967. The furniture and large boxes were brought to Col Alto. Two hundred barrels and cartons of porcelain were stored in the basement of the Student Union building and later moved to the basement of the Reserve Officer Training Corps building.

Until an appropriate facility at Washington and Lee became available for exhibiting the collection, special items as suggested by Dol were to be displayed in the Lee Chapel Museum on the front campus of the university. Built in the late 1860s when General Robert E. Lee was president of what was then named Washington College, it served as a chapel, General Lee's office, and at his death, a tomb. Members of his immediate family were buried in the crypt adjacent to his office. Later his father, General "Light Horse Harry" Lee would be reinterred near his son.

The arrival on campus of the largest moving van in Allied's fleet raised yet again for some the question that had nagged us since the beginning: "Why does Washington and Lee need all these dishes?" I had no immediate answer, but as the university's treasurer, I knew that 200 barrels of anything had value. Mrs. Reeves in her deed of gift made it clear that any item could be sold but only if the income was applied to the expenses of the collection.

An exhibit case for the Lee Chapel Museum was ordered to house the most valuable items. The brass plate on the case read:

The Reeves Collection
Given In Honor of
Mrs. Chester Green Reeves
And
Miss Lizzie Dyer

Priceless items of Americana were placed on view on May 1, 1967, two weeks after arriving in Lexington. For the most part, the case contained items I first saw in the dark, dank vault on my initial visit to 93. There were cups, saucers, plates, bowls, tea and coffee pots, all decorated with patriotic American symbols: ships flying the American flag, eagles inspired by the Great Seal of the United States, and monograms of American patriots. The "Hong Bowl," so highly prized by the Reeveses, had been purchased from one of the premiere dealers in Chinese export porcelain, Elinor Gordan of Villanova, Pennsylvania. Mrs. Gordon described the transaction:

> It was 1951 and I was participating in my first New York antiques show. The large punch bowl was placed in the most prominent position in my booth as a "show stopper."
>
> It was an extremely rare item dating to the 1785-1810 period. The decoration, with flags flying, depicted the warehouses or "hongs" where foreign nations dealt with the Chinese. The hongs were located in Canton along the Pearl River not far from Whampoa, the anchorage for the trading ships. The enclave, restricted to foreigners, served merchant ships from England, Bourbon France, Spain, Holland, Sweden and, after 1784, the United States of America.
>
> Mrs. Reeves, dressed in black with a long knitted coat, spotted the bowl and inquired of the price. I politely replied, "The bowl is not for sale. It belongs to my husband Horace." She in rapid order stated in a cultured, soft-spoken manner, "Mrs. Gordon, any item on display in this show *is* for sale. How much is the bowl?" Nervously I explained I would attempt to contact my husband who was in a business meeting in Philadelphia. Eventually reaching Horace I explained the dilemma.
>
> He gave me what I thought to be excellent advice: "This is your first major show, and it is important to establish an excellent reputation. Fix the price so outrageously high that she will not pursue the matter."
>
> Returning to the booth and screwing up all the courage at my command, I informed Mrs. Reeves that Mr. Gordon would sell the bowl, and the price was $1,500. Seemingly undaunted, she opened her black pigskin bag, retrieved a small change purse and handed me 15 one-hundred-dollar bills. The bowl was hers and became a valued part of the collection. I understand that she and Mr. Reeves left immediately by taxi for Grand Central Station and Mrs. Reeves held the bowl on her lap the entire train trip to Providence.

According to Mrs. Gordon, the exorbitant price of $1,500 in 1951 had appreciated to $125,000 fifty years later in 2001. The newly purchased Hong Bowl was a duplicate of the one I had seen at the John Brown house in early 1964 that originally belonged to Dol's great-great grandfather. The Reeveses' Hong Bowl may have been on one of Brown's ships upon its return from China to Providence more than 150 years before.

A number of dealers in American antiques who, like the Gordons, became the major supply sources of Louise and Euchlin Reeves' burgeoning collection had fascinating stories about the couple who sometimes feigned poverty, paid on the installment plan, endorsed stock dividend checks over to the seller and at times bartered for a special object. All agreed that the Reeves were a devoted couple, highly knowledgeable of the purchases they made and were dedicated to seeking fine specialized antique porcelains, furniture and silver.

David Stockwell, a noted antiques dealer, praised their professional acumen when they bought, on time, the three Chippendale chairs that belonged to George Washington during the period the nation's capital was located in Philadelphia.

Phillip Suval, a New York dealer, sold the Reeveses many Chinese export pieces with sailing ships flying the American flag. The large grouping of the ships they acquired became known as the "Reeves Armada." Millie Manheim of Manheim Galleries of New York catered to the Reeveses' pursuit of eighteenth-century English ceramic wares: pearlware, creamware and saltglaze.

Theodore Beckhardt of Antique Porcelain, also in New York, found for the Reeveses items with marks from early European factories in Germany, Austria and France. One of his most exciting finds for Mrs. Reeves was a large charger from the swan service, made at Meisen, that matched her platter which she had bought in Europe in the late 1890s.

Shreve, Crump & Low Antiques was a shop never missed on the couple's visits to Boston. Mrs. Phillip Hardy of Williams Street in Providence sought out and then sold American presidential items to the Reeveses. The Sack family and the firm of Ginsburg & Levy in New York stayed in close touch with Euc and Louise as valued collectors.

And so it went for twenty-five years, shop to shop, gallery to gallery, auction to auction, hand-in-hand Dol and Boy scanned every nook and cranny. Should they see one item in a large lot, they would buy the entire assortment. In doing so they would keep all the unimportant pieces — inexpensive plates, cups and saucers given as premiums at local movie theatres on Saturday nights, and dishes given with the purchase of gasoline added to their eclectic accumulation. Little did they realize that they were assembling a study collection of both fine and not-so-fine objects. David Stockwell would say, "A student should see the inferior in order to appreciate the superior." The Reeves Collection presented just such an opportunity.

Washington and Lee's honor system and its speaking custom have been two of the university's most prized traditions since General Lee's presidency in the late 1860s. On May 11, 1967, a beautiful spring day shortly after the collection arrived, I passed a couple walking along the Colonnade on the front campus. I spoke, and they returned my greeting.

The woman, in heavy woolen clothes, said, "You don't remember me." I confessed apologetically that she was correct. "I'm Mrs. Reeves' nurse, Beulah Anderson." Out of uniform and with her husband, she seemed different, but I quickly remembered.

"What brings you south to Virginia?" I asked. Mrs. Anderson, somewhat nervously replied, "Mrs. Reeves sent us here to see the porcelain."

The Colonnade and Lee Chapel face each other, so I suggested we view the exhibit case, which, by good fortune, had been installed the week before. As we walked toward the chapel, I inquired about Mrs. Reeves and was told they had taken her a week earlier to visit Mount Auburn Cemetery in Cambridge. It was the first spring day in Providence. After being lifted from her car, she placed six small stones and six crimson roses on Euchlin's simple marker. "Mrs. Reeves was very tired, and I don't believe she will be going back," Mrs. Anderson said.

Descending to the museum on the chapel's lower level, the Andersons viewed the porcelain that was on display. Admitting their limited knowledge, they were nonetheless impressed with its beauty. Beulah snapped several Polaroids for Mrs. Reeves. They returned to Providence on Saturday and went immediately to Ruth's Nursing Home to report to Dol on their trip to Washington and Lee.

Holding the pictures close to her eyes, her smile began to widen. This tiny, brave woman with the wispy white hair and the bright blue eyes had emotionally tied her life together with a neat ribbon. She had traveled to Cambridge to express her love to Boy at Mount Auburn and she was now assured that their treasures, lovingly collected over twenty-five years of marriage, were safe and secure.

Dol had a peaceful night's sleep. Early the next morning, Sunday, May 14, 1967, Louise Herreshoff Reeves died at the age of ninety-one.

Robbie delivered to the mortician the "Merry Christmas" plastic bag containing Dol's gray silk dress. It had been hanging in the vestibule of 89 for nearly four years. Fannie added a bright scarf. A picture of Boy taken in front of 89 and given to Dol at the time of his death was placed in the casket at her side. The silver bracelet with the Eiffel Tower charm, a gift from her beloved niece, Frances Reeves, remained on her left wrist.

Tuesday, May 16, was a bright, beautiful day, the sun shining on the blossomed trees and the flowering plants of Mount Auburn Cemetery. It contrasted sharply with that bleak and snowy day four months earlier, when Boy was buried.

Long-stemmed crimson colored roses draped the casket as it was placed at the foot of the John Dyer obelisk on the left side of the three stone steps. Aunt Lizzie, entombed forty years before, was nearby. The cortege of four vehicles lined the horseshoe bend on Willow Avenue. I joined the Reeves family from South Carolina and Dol's closest relatives, Norman Herreshoff and Louise DeWolf, as the Reverend Owings Stone from St. John's Episcopal Church performed the burial service.

Dol at ninety-one and Boy at sixty-three were side by side in their fragile union again as they had been for twenty-five years.

CHAPTER

10

A COLLECTION
IN SEARCH OF A HOME

The deaths of Euchlin and Louise Herreshoff Reeves in
1967 seemed at first to close the personal side of the
gift made to Washington and Lee University. In reality,
it was a beginning.

Several changes in the administration of the university
occurred within a year of the arrival of the Reeves Collection. Fred Carrington Cole resigned as president to become
director of the Council on Library Resources in Washington;
William Webb Pusey III, dean of the college, was named acting
president; and soon Robert Edward Royall Huntley, then dean
of the school of law, was elected president. These three scholars gave the establishment of the Reeves Collection their full
support. The faculty, for the most part, were less enthusiastic.
Some were outspokenly critical.

A few professors appreciated the collection's historical
and esthetic value, and their interest and support raised student awareness of the unusual study resource as it related to
their respective disciplines. Gradually increasing in number
over the years, students would come from the foreign language, English, history, anthropology, archaeology, chemistry,

commerce, religion and art departments, and from the School of Law.

Pieces of furniture from the Reeves Collection were selected from storage at Col Alto to be used in Lee House, the university president's residence. The stately home had been built for General Lee during his presidency. A hundred years later, while not completely lacking, it was in serious need of appropriate pieces of furniture in keeping with its historic nature and specialized use. Artisans and craftsmen from the university's maintenance staff exhibited new skills as they set about to repair, restore, refinish and reupholster the furniture.

The large Charleston ballroom mirror from the foyer of 93 Benevolent received new gold leaf and was placed in the entrance hall of the house, reflecting an eighteenth-century Pembroke table with arched stretcher, flanked by a pair of ornately carved English Chippendale side chairs. A hand-painted American Hepplewhite tea table with two caned-shield-back matching chairs, all in satinwood, also graced the foyer. An American drop-leaf mahogany table with claw-and-ball feet, and a Connecticut knee-hole desk with original brasses, both pieces from the eighhteenth century, complemented the existing furniture.

In the dining room a large gold-framed mirror that reached from the black marble mantle top to the twelve-foot ceiling was used with a transitional highboy dating to the William and Mary and the Queen Anne periods. A crown molding of the highboy concealed a secret drawer for holding maps or other important documents in the 1700s. The American Chippendale chairs that came from George Washington's home in Philadelphia were placed beside the tilt-top mahogany table from the Connecticut home where, by tradition, General Washington and the Comte de Rochambeau in 1781 planned the siege of Yorktown. An early American sterling tea service was placed on the table. These highly important items formed a grouping in the alcove of the room in which General Lee had died in October 1870.

The library and the music room were furnished with items from both the eighteenth and nineteenth centuries: a large drop-leaf walnut table, an oversized flame mahogany linen press with a desk drawer, an English Chippendale card table, a Victorian settee with matching lady's and gentleman's chairs, and a South Carolina marble-top center table. Bell-metal candlesticks, a pair of large pale yellow Sèvres vases, Chinese celadon garden seats of palest green, and numerous forms of nineteenth-century Rose Medallion porcelain completed the ground-floor accents in Lee House.

Following the collection's arrival on campus, unpacking, washing and sorting the ceramics became the seemingly endless task at hand. Two rooms in the basement of the university's Reserve Officer Training Corps building were made available for the ceramics. Pressed-wood composition shelving, extending from floor to ceiling, lined the walls. Aisles were created with open cases throughout the rooms. A large sink with rubber insulation to protect the fragile objects was installed, with carpeting covering the floors to soften an accidental mishap.

Two hundred large cartons and barrels were moved from the Student Union, where they had been temporarily stored, to the new site. The furniture from the Reeveses' home not placed in Lee House, as well as the old frames from the attic in Providence, stayed in storage at the unoccupied Col Alto mansion. We opened one barrel at a time.

Mrs. Tabbut, the president's housekeeper, earned extra income in the evenings by carefully washing the ceramics, piece after piece. My wife, Celeste, dried each object, handing it on to me for placement on a shelf. With evenings free from my responsibilities as university treasurer and secretary of the board of trustees, we were unencumbered of our usual chores. In the confines of the narrow aisles the three of us became as proficient in our responsibilities, and as dependent upon each other's movements, as a trio of mimes performing a silent ballet.

Surrounded by the collection during those nights of pleasurable labor, we witnessed a transformation of the objects we held. The years of accumulated dust that turned to dirt disappeared to reveal brilliant, jewel-like colors of the intricate and artistic decorations.

When the Reeveses had purchased an item, they placed it in the most convenient space available, and seldom was it moved again. Items that matched could well have been in separate rooms or stored in separate houses. As a consequence, rarely, if ever, were a matching cup and saucer unpacked and cleaned at the same time. There was no grouping of barrels by type or quality of the piece we were handling; they were identified only by the room from which they had come in either 89 or 93 Benevolent Street.

An unprofessional analysis, after working with the collection week after week, was quite simple: the Reeveses' passion for assembling the finest, the good and the not so good, was their conviction, a way to feel immortal. Cloistered, surrounded by tangible links to generations long since passed, they, too, felt ageless.

It was understandable for the pair to believe that objects they were buying for large sums of money had, 200 years before, cost only a fraction of their current price. Why not then expect the ceramics to continue increasing in desirability and value? In 1786 George Washington paid approximately $150 for his 300-piece dinner service for use at Mount Vernon — just under fifty cents per piece for that set of Chinese export porcelain with the decoration of the Society of the Cincinnati. It would increase in value over the years to several thousand dollars per item. By no means does this imply that the Reeves believed all their purchases would realize similarly dramatic appreciation. And if they did or did not, it was of no moment, for they had the pleasure and excitement that came with the hunt, the find, the purchase and especially the possession.

The process of unpacking and cleaning each fragile item continued for months, then beyond a year, and eventually into 1969. As word spread of the boxes and barrels, a limited number of visitors and students found unexpected pleasure as they joined us and unwrapped an item or two, uncovering a teacup or plate of historic or artistic merit. Through this process, a number of new friends became exposed to the Reeves Collection housed in the crowded rooms of a basement in the university's R.O.T.C. building. One barrel, partially unpacked, was purposely set aside to satisfy the curiosity of our guests. Most considered it, and rightfully so, a distinct honor to unwrap a piece or two.

A detective game of sorts began as we assembled items from the same service, identifying the country of origin and the manufacturer. Excitement filled the room when the cover of a tureen with an armorial coat of arms matched and fit a bowl or base unpacked and placed on a shelf several weeks or months before. The same was true of matching a cup with its saucer, or finding the warm-milk creamer that completed an English, French or Chinese tea set.

Our fingers running over various pieces guided the first sorting procedure. Some items were smooth to the touch, others were gritty. Some were feather-light, others heavy. Holding an object to a strong light, we could determine its translucency or its opaqueness. Later in the sorting process, items with underglaze decorations were separated from the overglaze pieces and from those decorated in a transfer process. There was milk-glass copying porcelain, porcelain copying silver and other combinations in the barrels. Many ceramic pieces were models of clay, metal or wooden forms taken by ship captains to the Orient for porcelain replicas — silver tea caddies, pots, creamers, sugars, punch bowls, cider flagons, pitchers and shaving bowls. The small tea bowl was a Chinese form, and when enlarged it became a soup bowl. When expanded to the clay and kiln's limit, the small teacup dictated the shape of a large punch bowl. The proper combination of the Chinese clay kaolin and petunse fired in kilns made the resonance possible. Lightly tapped true hard-paste porcelain would, as a bell, ring with a perfect tone.

The variations in form and decoration assisted in the initial stage of separating and placing items on the shelves. Not long into the process, we realized professional guidance was essential, and a visit to the ceramic collection division at the Smithsonian Institution in Washington was our first stop. Enthusiastically, Jefferson Miller III, the associate director of ceramics and glass, volunteered to come to the university and spend time culling and sorting. Jeff was amazed at the volume and variety of the collection. He worked with the Chinese export items made for the American market, while sharing information he had collected in independent study in Maryland and later at the Smithsonian. Trained as a lawyer, Jeff gave up the bar for antique ceramics. It was a transition I could not understand in my early days of working with "the dishes," but over time I would understand. We developed a real friendship, and I called on Jeff's assistance many times in subsequent years.

John Austin, curator of ceramics at Colonial Williamsburg, provided the same professional assistance with the eighteenth-century English creamware, pearlware and salt-glaze items. He would remark how helpful it was to compare the English ceramics with the products of other countries and continents. At Williamsburg the archaeological finds were primarily English in origin.

Elise and Henry Clay Hofheimer of Norfolk, Virginia, spent untold hours with the Dr. John Wall–period porcelains from the Worcester factory in England. It was enlightening to hear at times a disagreement among the experts as they were able to date a creamer or a bowl within one or two years of its manufacture in the mid-eighteenth century.

Elinor and Horace Gordon of Villanova, Pennsylvania — the couple who sold the Hong Bowl to the Reeveses — were dealers in choice Chinese export porcelain. They would find many "old friends" in the R.O.T.C. basement: items they had sold to the Reeveses. They added much to the historical provenance of countless objects. American market pieces made in China, circa 1785 to 1815, with eagles, flags and ship decorations were their specialty. From the Gordons I heard for the first time *"caveat emptor,"* or "let the buyer beware," in the context of antiques and the decorative arts. Fakes or imitations could easily fool the untrained eye. Placing a spurious item among originals became a teaching tool as the collection developed into a study and research program. The counterfeit object was valuable in the learning process.

The wealth of knowledge, freely given by new-found friends brought to the basement of the R.O.T.C. building over several years, cannot be easily calculated. For the most part, these experts and connoisseurs were visiting Lexington for the first time.

Among them was David Sanctuary Howard of Heirloom and Howard, London, universally recognized as the premier authority on Chinese armorial porcelain. He visited Lexington on his frequent trips to the United States. David could spot a coat of arms at thirty paces and give the history of the families that were identifiable by the crest and the quarterings. English history with a touch of seventeenth- and eighteenth-century gossip was being taught not in a history classroom, but in the basement of a concrete block building. No visit to England by collectors of Chinese export was complete without a visit with David Howard.

At about the time the collection arrived at Washington and Lee, Elizabeth and William Watson of Lynchburg, Virginia, had returned after living in the Orient for three decades. As an alumnus of the university, William Watson and his wife, known to all as "E," were inveterate collectors of fine porcelains made in China and Japan. Their close association with the Reeves Collection and the students with whom they worked and traveled later would inspire the creation of the Watson Pavilion for East Asian Studies, a major study and exhibit center adjacent to the Reeves Center, with support for the pavilion and an endowed professorship in East Asian Studies.

The collection brought to the campus individuals who were theretofore unknown to the university, and usually vice versa. Without exception, the experience of unpacking the objects, never knowing what treasure the protective wrappings might hold — regional pottery, twentieth-century Willow Ware or a fragile teacup of delicate eggshell porcelain — inspired an ongoing dedication by the visitors to the program that was evolving.

David Stockwell of Wilmington, Delaware, identified American furniture of the eighteenth century as well as porcelains from the Orient and continental Europe. Crosby Forbes of the Museum of the China Trade in Milton, Massachusetts, later with the Peabody-Essex Museum in Salem, a descendant of early traders with China, was helpful in all aspects of "the treasures from Cathay." Later he was joined by his associate, William Sargent, who never failed to assist when the provenance or identity of a particular piece was in question.

From London came John Cushion and, later, John Ayers, both formerly of the Victoria and Albert Museum. Cushion devoted his time to ceramics from a plethora of factories throughout England; Ayers concentrated on the limited number of blanc de chine (white porcelain) figures. The beautifully modeled examples were from the kilns of the Fukien area in China where stark white clay was found.

Letitia Roberts, a true porcelain scholar from Sotheby's in New York, helped with the identification process and was always available to students and to me, by telephone or in person, to assist in the interpretation of decorations and manufacturers' marks.

While still with Christie's in London, Anthony du Boulay, James Godfrey and Ian Kennedy visited the Washington and Lee campus and identified porcelains, furniture and silver in the collection. Hardly an antique of note in all areas of the decorative arts went unnoticed by the experienced eyes of this trio.

There was something about the accumulation in the basement rooms that both fascinated and challenged the knowledge of experts. Surprise lit the faces of many as the eclectic objects of art were unwrapped. Close friendships developed over the years with a large number of formerly "one-time strangers" who opened barrels, climbed ladders to top shelves or, on bended knee, plied through stack after stack of dishes.

11

WORLDWIDE PROMINENCE AND ONE JITTERY NIGHT AT HOME

By word of mouth the Reeves Collection began to gain recognition beyond the basement of the R.O.T.C. building. After viewing the collection, Georgians Joseph E. Birnie of Atlanta and Joseph L. Lanier Sr. of West Point, members of the Washington and Lee board of trustees, introduced me to Gudmand Vigtel, director of Atlanta's High Museum. He, in turn, offered to mount an exhibit of the China trade porcelain from the Reeves Collection. Kitty Gross Farnham and Callie Huger Efird, museum curator and volunteer respectively, agreed to research the collection and write the exhibition catalogue. In the crowded basement they photographed and wrote descriptions of 277 choice items.

The experience of watching two trained scholars while they sorted, selected, and researched an item, using the collection's limited library, then photographing and developing a layout, was a learning experience that would serve me well in another area of the collection — at the time not known to me but realized two years later.

The exhibition, the catalogue and the opening-night reception at the High Museum in Atlanta in 1973 would bring national attention to the Reeves Collection and highlight a hidden treasure at Washington and Lee.

That same year, Wendell Garrett, editor of *The Magazine Antiques,* featured the Reeves Collection with five pages of color photographs in the October issue.

Sponsored by the Smithsonian Institution and later by the university, the High Museum exhibit traveled to museums in twenty-seven states and the District of Columbia.

In 1978 Dr. I-Hsiung Ju, professor and artist-in-residence at Washington and Lee, arranged to have an exhibition of specially selected Reeves Collection items mounted at the National Museum of History in Taipei, Taiwan. The exhibition was uniquely and beautifully displayed in galleries bordering a lake covered in blooming pink lotus, a flower seen often in Chinese decorations. Every object was displayed separately, with a Chinese scroll of silk or rice paper behind it in the case to emphasize the porcelain's color and decoration. Specimens of trade porcelain — ordered by the "foreign flag devils" and exported 200 years before from the hongs along the Pearl River in Canton to satisfy Western tastes — had seldom been kept and thus had previously been seen only centuries ago by those Chinese who were directly involved in the trade. To their descendants, viewing the artistry of their ancestors was a rare and, at times, enthralling experience.

◆

The general unrest on college campuses in the late 1960s and early 1970s did not spare Washington and Lee. Unlike a number of institutions of higher education, however, students at the university engaged in dialogue rather than violence, maintaining an atmosphere of subdued concern, as morning newspapers reported the burning of R.O.T.C. buildings in various parts of the country every day. Word reached Washington and Lee President Robert E. R. Huntley that Washington and Lee's military building might well be a target for vandals from outside the area. In addition to the harm that could come to the university, the Reeveses' life work was also in danger in the R.O.T.C. basement.

From noon to midnight on the day of the suspected vandalism, four of us — William "Bub" Mohler, the university purchasing agent; James Kirkland, my close associate and superintendent of the maintenance staff; my wife, Celeste; and I — repacked 50 barrels of the rarest items in the collection. We used varied and sometimes-unorthodox wrapping materials—newspapers, cleaning cloths and anything suitable at hand. Mr. Kirkland then transported the hurriedly packed boxes in his pickup truck to a secure off-campus site.

As the first truck left the R.O.T.C. building just after dark, a group of Washington and Lee students, rifles under arm, surrounded the building. They were there to shield the campus headquarters of military training, and in doing so performed double duty by protecting the Reeves Collection. Their vigilance was never adequately acknowledged. To those students who were there during those frightening nights, I take this opportunity to express the deepest appreciation possible. Their actions may have saved more than a building with symbolic meaning but also tangible links to the birth of their university and our nation.

CHAPTER

12

AN EXPLOSION
OF COLOR

With the curtailment of the collection's travel schedule, there was time to return to Col Alto, the house where the Reeveses' furniture had been placed before much of it was moved to the Lee House. Also, it was there that the miscellaneous cartons were stored that contained the old frames that were taken from the attic of 93 Benevolent.

Removing the tape from one of the sealed cartons, I unwrapped a black wooden frame, two feet by three, surrounding a pane of heavy glass. Surely, I thought, it must contain a faded black-and-white print, or possibly a steel engraving. The subject was completely obscured by nearly an inch of accumulated gray powder that clung to the glass. With a hand-towel soaked in water, I wiped across the center of the framed glass, turning the dust to a thin sludge.

Doing so quite accidentally loosed an explosion of color. It was a painting of multicolored flowers. The thick oils were brilliant reds . . . vivid greens . . . magenta . . . yellow . . . deep shades of blue . . . and many hues in between. The flowers appeared wet as though the pigments were applied that very day. But that was impossible! Never had I seen the likes of the variety of thick strokes of jumbled paint.

AN EXPLOSION OF COLOR

Had it not been for a signature in one corner, "Louise Eaton" printed in black, it would have been difficult to know the top from the bottom. On the reverse of the frame was a piece of paper glued to a backing of aged blue-and-white mattress ticking. The striped cloth was barely distinguishable; it too, was covered in layers of gray dust. Carefully removing the title written on fragile paper, the word "Poppies" became visible. Poppies? I had no reason to question the description by the artist. But the signature — who was Louise Eaton?

Intrigued by the painting and the questions it posed, I unpacked another frame from the box and applied the same crude dust-removal technique. This time I was looking through the glass to a watercolor of pale shades of orange and blue. I could see no definite form, but it, too, looked as though it had been recently painted. There was no sign of a signature, and I was not quite sure if I might be holding it upside down. After wiping the thick dusty powder from three or four other frames all different in subject and technique, I thought it best to have someone with knowledge of art take a look.

Marion Junkin, chairman of the university's fine arts department, was an artist himself, and I felt confident he could recognize the style, if not the signatures. "This is a Fauvist painting," was his immediate remark. "Who painted it?"

"Fauvist" meant nothing to me; nor could I answer his question as to the artist's identity. Nevertheless, I was determined to learn the answers to both. Professor Junkin asked if there were more, and over a period of several weeks, we worked together to clear away dust from twenty or more of the paintings. Marion described each painting one-by-one as it was unpacked: academic, Expressionist, Fauvist, Impressionist, Post-Impressionist, sketch, unfinished, plein-air, bold and impastoed.

The signatures on the paintings were as diverse as the art: L. H. Eaton; Louise; L. E.; L. Herreshoff; L. C. H.; Herreshoff; L.C. Eaton; L. Eaton; Louise Herreshoff Eaton.

One of the larger frames held the portrait of an elderly woman that, at first glance, I thought must have been the one I had seen in the living room of the "little museum" at 93 Benevolent during my first visit there with Mr. Reeves. Though the subject was the same, the painting under glass seemed unfinished. The box contained three similar treatments of the same subject. They were clearly not portraits of Mrs. Reeves, as I had guessed on that eventful afternoon in 1964; in no way did they resemble Dol.

Professor Junkin was fascinated and studied the portraits carefully. One was signed with the initials "L. E.," and on the back, written on the mattress ticking were the words "Portrait of My Aunt Elizabeth." Was this Elizabeth Dyer, who was named in the deed of gift? If so, then who was "L. E."?

My first call was to Euchlin's sister-in-law, Fannie Reeves, in Charleston, South Carolina. She knew immediately the initial "E."

"Dol was married to a Charles Eaton, and carried the name until she married Euchie," Fannie explained. The mystery was solved in part, but I thought I should check with Louise DeWolf, Dol's cousin in Bristol, Rhode Island.

"Yes, Cousin Louise had been an artist and was married to Charles Eaton," Louise DeWolf told me. Then she volunteered, "He was her third cousin." I explained the reason for my call but further information about Louise, Eaton or the name Herreshoff was not forthcoming.

In time Louise DeWolf would become my principal source of information, as well as an enjoyable friend to Celeste and me. Why had Euc never mentioned the paintings during the years that we worked together on the porcelain?

AN EXPLOSION OF COLOR

During a telephone conversation Donald Delahunt could add little to enlighten me about either the paintings or Louise's marriage to Charles Eaton. He made an interesting point when he explained the delay in Euchlin's funeral on January 13, four days after his death: It was to remove "Eaton" from Mrs. Reeves' tombstone that had been placed there fifty years earlier. Delahunt could not, or chose not to, elaborate on their earlier lives.

Fannie Reeves read me the obituary for Dol that appeared in the Providence *Evening Bulletin.* It provided valuable clues about the collector and painter.

As the project of unpacking the framed paintings continued, Professor Junkin concluded that to assess them properly, they should be removed from the frames and glass. The explosion of color that I experienced with *Poppies* under glass became even more dramatic as held the painting in direct sunlight. The flowers came almost literally to life, and I began to see and appreciate the beauty of art as I never had before.

Researching the Reeves porcelain collection had been possible through published materials and the assistance of scholars in the field of ceramics. The paintings, however, presented an entirely different conundrum. No one, it seemed, really knew Mrs. Reeves as an artist. Louise DeWolf, her cousin, had seen a portrait of a lady in a home in Bristol that she believed had been painted by Cousin Louise. Norman Herreshoff, Dol's nephew, remembered seeing, many years before, a portrait by his aunt of a small boy leaning against a tree. The painting was in the New York City home of Louise's father, Dr. J. B. Freancis Herreshoff, Norman's grandfather. With the exception of Louise DeWolf and Norman Herreshoff, no one I met during my three-year association with Mr. Reeves or during the four months that I knew Mrs. Reeves could shed any light on the paintings. Next-door neighbors were not aware that Louise had been an artist, nor were the Reeveses' friends in the ceramic circles.

How best to proceed with the new-found collection of paintings? After unpacking nearly a hundred of the frames, a proper method for further cleaning and study had to be found. A non-professional answer involved chicken-wire and wide picture shelves. The university's buildings-and-grounds staff was asked to cover several walls in the upstairs bedrooms of Col Alto with the unorthodox materials. With metal hooks attached to wire on the reverse side of the paintings, it was possible to mount the paintings after we had cleaned off the dust. Removing the glass could happen later.

As with the initial sorting of the porcelain, I attempted to group the paintings by subject: portraits, flowers, seascapes, boats, porcelain, trees, fields. Later I would regroup them by style as first described to me by Marion Junkin: Fauvist, Impressionist, plein-air, and so forth. Because the time I found to spend with the paintings was mostly at night, a spotlight borrowed from the university drama department helped me find signatures and appreciate the beauty of color.

A number of the paintings carried Louise's married name, Eaton, and I was quite sure the works had been painted after 1910, the year of her unfortunate marriage. My theory was later disproved as I discovered that, while Louise may not have loved her husband, for some unknown reason, she liked his name. Louise even added "Eaton" to paintings she made during her childhood and teenage years.

One evening in 1970, during a weekend meeting of Washington and Lee's board of trustees, I asked one of the members, an avid collector and a true lover of art, to accompany me to the old, dark, uninhabited Col Alto mansion. On a pretense, now long forgotten, we ascended the winding stair-case to the chicken-wire gallery. We stayed until daylight.

Jonathan Westervelt Warner of Tuscaloosa, Alabama, was my companion. Jack, his wife, Elizabeth, and the Warner Foundation of the Gulf States Paper Company, of which he was then chief executive and chairman, own one of the truly great private collections of American fine and decorative arts. After studying the art for some time, Jack gave me much-needed encouragement to continue researching the paintings.

I remember Jack standing in front of the painting of the elderly woman, the work I had seen on my first visit to the Reeveses' "little museum."

"Does it have a title?" he asked.

"Yes. It's called *A Portrait of My Aunt Elizabeth*."

As we descended from the second floor and left Col Alto, Jack, as an afterthought, turned to me and murmured, "Everybody has an Aunt Lizzie."

I realized then he had seen much deeper than the surface of the portrait. Our evening began an art friendship that has lasted more than thirty years. Later Jack Warner would give Washington and Lee the portrait presented to the Bengali merchant Ramdoolal Dey in 1803 by American seamen. It was returned to the United States after hanging in steamy Calcutta for more than 150 years.

Other alumni and friends would come to see the Herreshoff paintings exhibited in this unique manner. Not all were as excited as I. One looked me straight in the eye and said, "And you expect to make a silk purse from a sow's ear?" This blunt-speaking young man, Robert Keefe, director of university communications, was eventually to become one of the most helpful individuals in bringing positive attention to Louise Herreshoff's art.

On business and personal trips to New York, Celeste and I would take two or three of the smaller paintings and walk from gallery to gallery on 57th Street and up and down Madison Avenue. The answer was always the same: "We're not interested in unknown artists — and certainly not unknown *women* artists."

We had plunged headfirst into a sophisticated and foreign world, and without a change of tactics we would have soon drowned.

Entering one gallery, Hirschl & Adler, between Madison and Fifth Avenues, we approached the young man behind the receptionist's desk and politely introduced ourselves as being with Washington and Lee University and asked if the gallery appraised paintings.

"Yes, we do," he said. "Who is the artist?"

In a steady tone I replied, "I should have said *artists,*" and added, without emotion, "We wish an appraisal of a Charles Willson Peale, a Gilbert Stuart and a Wollaston or two." Indeed the university owned an impressive collection, bequeathed largely by the Lee family.

We had made an impression. He raised his head and, with a quizzical expression, looked directly at us for the first time. "Please express the paintings you wished appraised to . . . ."

But before he could complete the sentence, I said, "They are not permitted to leave the campus."

At that instant, I felt a tap on my shoulder, and a distinguished-looking gentleman with a soft-spoken voice, unlike any we had heard that day, said "I'm Norman Hirschl, and I will be delighted to come to Lexington and appraise the paintings you mention. There will be no charge except for my travel costs."

Was I dreaming, and had I breached the university honor code? I decided I was innocent on both charges. After all, as university treasurer, I was responsible for getting the university's most valuable assets appraised for insurance purposes. A mutually agreeable date was set, and Celeste and I

Plate 1: *Sarah Unfinished*
1898

*All paintings from the collection of the Reeves Center,
Washington and Lee University*

Plate 2: *Miss "T."*
1897

Plate 3: *Miss Edith Howe*
1897

Plate 4: *Le Répos*
1899

Plate 5: *An Interior*
1899

Plate 7: *Pink Azalea*
c. 1920

Opposite

Plate 6: *Girl in Garden*
1899

Plate 8: *In a Minor Key — Rockport*
c. 1921

Plate 9: *Weathered Boats — Rockport*
c. 1924

Plate 10: *Seascape*
c. 1910

Plate 11: *The Blue Ocean*
c. 1924

Plate 12: *Summertime Girl*
c. 1920

Plate 13: *Sword Lilies*
c. 1920

Plate 14: *Portrait of My Aunt Elizabeth*
c. 1926

left the gallery, never once mentioning a woman artist named Herreshoff.

Norman Hirschl arrived in Lexington and spent an entire day with the eighteenth-century paintings and provided important information and history about each. Having learned before his arrival of his prominence in the world of art both as a dealer and as a highly respected art historian, we set about planning a luncheon in his honor. An afternoon cocktail party for a few guests before his return to New York, we thought, would help define "Southern hospitality."

I never hinted at my ulterior motive and the true purpose of my invitation to Hirschl before we left for cocktails. Stopping by my office in Washington Hall, the center building on the National Historic Landmark–designated campus, he noticed several small paintings on the picture rail.

"Who is the artist?" he asked. "Louise Herreshoff, a turn-of-the-century woman from Providence," I replied.

He bit! "They're charming! Are there more?"

"Yes," I replied, trying not to give myself away. "Would you like to see them?"

We were off to the R.O.T.C. basement, where I had placed a single portrait in the pitch-black room. A spotlight was aimed directly at it, waiting to be lighted on my cue. Opening the door I flipped the light switch and there in all her colorful glory, wild blue eyes, bright red lips, and black dress, lace collar with the heart-shaped diamond brooch and open Oriental fan was Aunt Lizzie staring at Norman Hirschl. Her haunting eyes followed his every move.

"My God! As fine as a Bellows!"

◆

CHAPTER

13

A LILY-WHITE SPORT

Hearing Norman Hirschl's exclamation confirmed my belief in the artistic talent of Louise Herreshoff. It was not my knowledge of art that provided the drive to explore her works; I was as ignorant of the world of fine arts as I had been of the world of ceramics. It was a dual desire to bring to light these extraordinary paintings, hidden away for forty years in a dark and gloomy attic, and to seek recognition for their unknown creator. Fixed in my mind was the memory of the two bitter cold days in January 1967, when Louise gathered strength at the age of ninety-one, after years in a nursing-home bed, to attend her husband's funeral. Her bright, colorful, often sad, early years sprang forth on canvas in every stroke of her brush.

Norman Hirschl opened doors in a strata, at least for me, of an unknown world. Placing twenty of the Herreshoff paintings in the back of a Pontiac station wagon, I drove to museums and galleries in Philadelphia, New York and Washington, to which Hirschl had called ahead. The response, entirely because of his endorsement, was always polite, but noncommittal: "Interesting," "evocative," "ahead of her time."

None committed to an exhibition; most of the museum galleries and programs were booked two and three years ahead. Even so, Louise's paintings were being seen in a world unknown to her since *Le Répos* was selected for the Paris Salon in 1900.

Essteemed by most art critics and historians, Adelyn D. Breeskin of the National Portrait Gallery in Washington was a star in her field. Norman Hirschl obtained an appointment for us with her.

Arriving at the gallery, I was met by an unexpectedly mature but elegant woman. Every gray hair atop her high forehead was brushed back and straight, complementing her cultured voice, sharp and crisp. "Good morning, Mr. Whitehead. Please place the paintings against the wall around the room."

I nervously obeyed, attempting to arrange them in what I thought to be their chronological order. Not a word was said as she walked slowly from portraits, to seascapes, to flowers. On the way to Washington I had said several times to the paintings in the rear of the station wagon, "I can get you to the gallery, but it's up to you to make the sale."

Mrs. Breeskin retraced her steps, then said, "Come this way."

I followed her into one of the great marble halls of the gallery and she pointed to spaces occupied by portraits of great Americans. "The four *Aunt Lizzies* will hang here, *Girl in Garden* over there, I think the seascapes will work well above the stair case," she said.

Was I breathing? Had my heart stopped? Could I be hearing Dol's voice from above directing the placement of her paintings?

Attempting to show by my demeanor that I expected nothing less and at the same time attempting to remain upright, I heard Mrs. Breeskin say, "We will give Herreshoff an exhibition. I understand from Mr. Hirschl that Washington and Lee will produce a catalogue. I will confirm this conversation in writing and the dates for the show upon the return of the director later this week."

While I had driven them to Washington, the Herreshoff paintings sold themselves.

I immediately called Celeste and Professor Junkin in Lexington from a pay telephone booth just outside the gallery with the exciting news. I then sat down on a bench at the main entrance to the National Portrait Gallery and ate a bag of popcorn, one kernel at a time.

How far we had come, I thought to myself, from an earlier visit by a Washington art dealer shortly after the paintings were uncovered. I remembered her words to me vividly, "At most, the paintings are worth $12.50 each — frames included." Later she wrote Professor Junkin and offered to buy them all.

I thought back, too, on two days in June 1969. Celeste, our son, Paul, and I drove to Rhode Island to attend the United States Navy commissioning ceremony of our other son, Jim, at Newport. After checking into the Biltmore Hotel in nearby Providence, I drove to Benevolent Street to see if the old houses were still there, the ones I had visited on my first meeting with Mr. Reeves in early 1964. Robbie Reeves, who inherited the houses, had sold them soon after Louise died. There they were; in the warm, summer sunshine, they appeared so different than they had that icy morning five years earlier.

Parking my car behind an old pickup truck, I knocked on the door of 89, the small wood-shingled residence. There was no answer and no sign of life. Walking next door to 93, the Reeveses' "little museum," I found the front door with all its Yale locks partially open. There was a loud noise from the inside, metal striking metal. "Anybody home?" I called out.

More loudly, "Anybody here?" After several attempts, a middle-aged man, covered in soot and looking like a handyman for the Mafia, came to the door.

"Whaddya want?" he asked.

I explained that I was from Virginia and had known the former occupants of the two houses. He, in turn, explained that the new owner had given him everything in the house to clean it out. Removing radiators, I realized, had intoned the awful racket that greeted me.

Standing just inside the front door now, I could see piled high, floor to ceiling in the small living room, old shutters, mattresses, and a nondescript assortment of junk. At the bottom of the heap that covered most of the room, I spotted a frame, about three feet wide by a foot high. As best I could make out, it was a photograph of the student body, made in front of the Colonnade on Washington and Lee's front campus.

Euc Reeves must be in the picture. "Will you sell me that photograph there?" I asked.

"Whaddya want it for?" he replied gruffly. I explained my friendship with Mr. Reeves. "A buck," he said. I gladly handed him a dollar bill.

The photograph had balanced a myriad of debris that tumbled to the floor when I bent down and pulled it out. Behind and above the mattresses and shutters were a number of frames I immediately recognized as mates to the Herreshoff paintings in Lexington. What lay beneath the dust-covered glass, whether watercolors, oils or something else, was indistinguishable.

I managed to restrain my eagerness as I purchased with cash, one frame at a time. The junkman's price increased by exponential increments as I retrieved each newly purchased frame. Two hundred and sixty one dollars later, his pile of junk had turned to gold.

Scooping up the frames I also retrieved several small batches of old letters and miscellaneous bits and pieces of paper and yellowed photographs. I had spent every cent of cash I had. The junkman refused a check; a credit card was out of the question.

As I was about to leave, the happy salesman called to me, "I have four frames in my barn like the ones you bought. You might like to see them. Follow me, I live out on the road to Connecticut."

There was no way to decline such an invitation, as my mind raced in anticipation of what I was about to see. Then I remembered my family was at the hotel, expecting my return several hours earlier. Here I was following a dilapidated truck driven by a stranger out into the country. Heading out of Providence toward Connecticut I thought several times of turning around, and then the escalating anticipation would keep my eyes on the truck. The drive to the outskirts of Providence was probably shorter than it seemed at the time. Eventually we turned on a dirt driveway to a barn on a grassy knoll that appeared considerably cleaner than the newly self-appointed art dealer I was following.

Sure enough, he showed me four frames holding exquisite, delicate watercolors of small boats at dockside. They were Louise's.

"How much are you asking?" I asked.

Without hesitating, "$250." He knew he had a sure sale.

I was floored. I had no cash, having already given him my very last cent. I had no reason to believe that Washington and Lee would wire me $250 for four watercolors when the Reeves Collection had nearly a hundred already in storage, hanging on chicken wire, and the most ambitious appraisal totaled $12.50 a piece.

Walking away, which is what any good businessman would have done, was out of the question. I simply could not imagine leaving behind four of Louise's paintings in the hands of a junkman.

"I'll call you tomorrow night after I see my son in Newport," I said. He agreed. I knew full well there would be no competing prospect for the old paintings in the next twenty-four hours.

The next day found us in Newport, excited for our son Jim's commissioning ceremony into the U.S. Navy officer corps. During dinner, I asked Jim in private if he had $200 in cash on hand, knowing I could get a $50 advance on my American Express credit card at the motel. "Sure, Dad. I was given my uniform allowance this morning." What a great relief.

Returning to the motel after dinner, I left Celeste and Paul, our younger son, in the room and, under some thin pretense, made my way to the lobby. There I called the junkman on a pay phone.

"Yeah?" he answered.

"This is Jim Whitehead calling from Newport," I announced. "I will buy the four watercolors."

"Yeah ..." (I began to wonder if he knew any other word.)

"You said $250, right?" I asked.

"Yeah, $250 ... *each*"

"*Each?!*" I asked incredulously, my voice rising.

"Yeah, each," the junkman underscored.

Weak, I returned the receiver to the cradle and returned Jim's cash.

Relating the episode to Joe Lanier and John Newton Thomas, members of the university's board of trustees, over breakfast a few weeks later, Joe said, "I would have sent you the $250 had I known." Jack echoed the offer. Hindsight!

The four paintings at a barn on the road to Connecticut, I hope, found a good home, but it is doubtful that the junkman found a more appreciative prospect than I. These watercolors by Louise Herreshoff may still be in a barn or attic or a closet somewhere in New England, but I am certain the junkman never received the $1,000 he last asked of me.

Three days after my appointment at the National Portrait Gallery, Adelyn Breeskin telephoned to inform me that the gallery's director had looked at three of the color slides and had decided Louise Herreshoff had "not painted enough." There would be no exhibition. I sensed in Mrs. Breeskin's voice disappointment, but hardly as much as mine. After all, her judgment as both one of America's leading art historians and a nationally acclaimed authority on Mary Cassatt had been questioned and challenged.

When earlier disappointments caused concern on my part, Marion Junkin would attempt to cheer me up with the comment, "Compared to the world of art at any level, professional wrestling is a lily-white sport." How right he was.

CHAPTER

14

SHORT-LIVED
DISAPPOINTMENT

At some point along the way of my journey into the rarefied world of art, I met a freelance writer who at the time was a reporter for an antiques journal headquartered in Tuscaloosa, Alabama. The unusual story of the Reeves Collection fascinated Janet Green, especially its link with an archaeological dig then underway at the ruins of Liberty Hall Academy, which, founded in 1749 as Augusta Academy, had been one of the predecessors to Washington and Lee University. The dig was uncovering, among other things, a number of shards of eighteenth-century ceramics that matched items collected by the Reeveses.

Arriving in Lexington from her home in Northern Virginia, Ms. Green came prepared to spend a full day at the dig site with Professor John McDaniel, the university's anthropologist and archeologist. She knew nothing of Louise Herreshoff's paintings, but it was my principal reason for inviting her to campus.

With pad and pencil in hand, she had taken copious notes from the time she arrived. Following lunch (chicken salad on rye, Eskimo Pie and tea served in a cup that once belonged to Paul Revere), I asked if she would like to see some of the paintings that had come with the collection.

We entered the pitch-black basement, just as I had with Norman Hirschl several months earlier, and I flipped the spotlight to reveal the portrait of Aunt Lizzie. Within minutes, Green was on the telephone to Dorothy Phillips and Linda Simmons of the curatorial staff at the Corcoran Gallery in Washington. "You must see the paintings of Louise Herreshoff," Green exclaimed.

"Who?" came the reply.

In her reportorial manner, Green hurriedly and succinctly covered the salient points. Turning to me she asked, "When can you take examples to the Corcoran Gallery in Washington?"

"Tomorrow!" I answered, without hesitation. An 11 a.m. appointment was set. Robert Keefe and Rom Weatherman from the university's news office and I set out for Washington that same evening with twenty paintings in the back of a Washington and Lee van. We checked into the Hay-Adams Hotel. It was a hot July night, and the air conditioning was out in our hotel rooms. Repairing to the hotel's first-floor bar, the three of us refreshed ourselves with cold beer and the sounds of Eileen Kelly, resident chanteuse, who sang and played at a grand piano badly in need of tuning.

The next morning, our meeting at the Corcoran began with a familiar command. "Place the paintings against the wall around the room," Dorothy Phillips requested. She and Ms. Simmons walked from one painting to the next, speaking softly to each other. As we stood by nervously, self-consciously, we could just as easily have been at the Westminster Kennel Show or the Miss America contest.

"Roy Slade, the director, is in his office today. I'd like for him to see the paintings," Mrs. Phillips finally said, as Ms. Simmons gave us a smile that I took as approval.

"Good morning, gentlemen," Mr. Slade said, as he glanced around the walls. "It's my understanding that you will produce a catalogue with color photographs and host a reception for your alumni in the Washington area. Mrs. Phillips will give you available dates for the opening. The show will run from early October through most of November. We hope you will also display porcelain in the galleries from the Reeves Collection at the same time."

We shook hands. "Thank you for bringing Louise Herreshoff to our attention." Roy Slade left the room almost as quickly as he had entered it.

◆

The celebration of the centennial of the American Revolution had been nearing its conclusion in 1876 when Louise Chamberlain Herreshoff was born on November 29 in Brooklyn, New York. Now, exactly a hundred years later, during the nation's bicentennial, her paintings, until now primarily unknown, would be exhibited at the Corcoran Gallery of Art in Washington. I wrote in the catalogue:

> In many respects, Louise Herreshoff's life may have been "typical" of the lives of a great many young women in the world of art during the same period, both in the early stages of art training and through the productive years of her painting. One is hard put to name even a handful of American women at the turn of the century who were to become widely known and recognized on the merits of their paintings. Yet in the late 1800s, and for that matter into the twentieth century, young ladies, and especially those with families of means, were expected to take courses in painting, principally as an avocation — seldom as their life's work.
>
> Actively to pursue painting was an expensive undertaking, especially if the training were to include lessons abroad from private teachers and the academies. While Paris and its environs attracted many young women art students from America, others dared not venture to Europe who lacked the financial resources to live "in the manner" expected of young

ladies of the time. (One may conjecture that today's lifestyle would not present nearly as many of the barriers as seemed to prevail at the end of the last century.)

And money was not the only obstacle faced by young women artists. Would they be taken seriously by the salons, by the galleries, by their teachers, by the dealers — or, even, by their own families? Would family or local recognition satisfy their ambitions, with their paintings hanging in the parlor or in the library of their school or in the local museum; would they be placed in storage, to be dusted off from time to time, or not at all? Would family and friends be shocked at new techniques, "the latest" from Paris; or would the paintings serve only as a reminder of a wonderful and beautiful youthful experience?

Coincidentally, it was also one hundred years exactly since William W. Corcoran, for whom the Corcoran Gallery was named, made several important gifts to Washington College honoring the late presidency of General Robert E. Lee. A number of his influential friends followed suit.

Selection and preparation of the paintings to be exhibited, cleaning, framing, photographing and research, all had to be completed in three short months. Bulk framing materials, antique gold-painted wood and linen liners for each of eighty-eight paintings were ordered. The university's carpenter, Clyde Hartless, a talented craftsman, measured and framed each picture. No two were exactly the same size. The chicken wire gone, cleaned and uniformly framed, the Herreshoff paintings would "sing," as one critic later wrote.

Our budget for the black-tie reception for 300 was modest: $3,000, including beverages, which divided exactly to $10 a person. Ridgewells, Washington's finest caterer and the one recommended by the Corcoran, estimated $5,000 for an event that would not embarrass us. Again, I knew we were out of our league. The additional $2,000 came from Christine Hale Martin and James Bland Martin of Gloucester, Virginia, and the caterer, sympathetic to our plight, took on the challenge.

SHORT-LIVED DISAPPOINTMENT

James Powers, an interior designer with Heironimus Department Stores in Roanoke, agreed to take on floral decorations. Sixty dozen long-stemmed crimson roses, Dol's favorite flower, were ordered to decorate the entrance hall of the Corcoran. I researched and wrote the catalogue, while Thomas Bradshaw and Sally Mann created the color and black-and-white photographs. Messrs. Keefe and Weatherman worked with a Washington printing company to complete the catalogue.

The portrait of Edith Howe, painted by Louise in Philadelphia in 1897, would play an important role in that publication. We needed to photograph it, but it was owned at the time by the subject's daughter, Mrs. Marshall Fulton of Monkey Wrench Road in Bristol, Rhode Island. Learning later that the exhibition would be shown in a number of cities, Mrs. Fulton called with a wonderful offer and I quickly accepted.

"If you will have color photographs made for my eight children, I will give the painting to Washington and Lee University," she said. "Mother always wanted to travel!"

Opening night at the Corcoran was a grand affair, worthy of the Reeveses' paintings and porcelain. The guests entering the Corcoran's grand hall were in awe. The gallery had been transformed into a setting worthy of an Arabian sultan.

Serving tables were laden with flaming crepes, pyramids of exotic fruits, trays of decorated poached salmon, shrimp and oysters on the half shell. White and dark chocolate truffles with a variety of cream-filled finger-size cakes filled the dessert carts. Uniformed waiters served fine wines and other spirits in crystal goblets on silver trays. The light from hundreds of tall tapers fell softly on nearly a thousand crimson colored roses throughout the hall.

What a hundredth birthday party for Louise Herreshoff, an American artist discovered!

The reviews of the Herreshoff paintings validated all the hard work and many long hours by a cadre of faithful believers. Roy Slade, the Corcoran Gallery's director, wrote in the catalogue:

> The paintings of Louise Herreshoff are a revelation of her individuality, demonstrating an art that was modern in its time. She was aware of the innovation and inquiry of contemporary painters, and her own style changed over the years as she was influenced by the major painters of the day. From a predictably conservative, academic beginning, she became a more adventuresome and responsive painter.
>
> As a person, as a painter and as a collector, Louise Herreshoff was a fascinating individual. The exhibition is as interesting a story of an individual and her life as it is a group of works of art. As a collector, Louise Herreshoff with her husband, Euchlin D. Reeves, gathered an extraordinary collection of ceramic pieces. Her marriage, the death of her aunt, and her abrupt withdrawal from painting are but a few examples of rich details from her fascinating life.
>
> Her early work is academic and competent, showing genuine ability and accomplishment. Gradually, her paintings became more adventurous, and with free brush strokes and strong color she made impressions and images of life. A strong influence on her painting resulted from her study in Paris, where she came into contact with the major artists of the day. The influence of the Impressionists and Fauves comes through strongly with vivid color and bold strokes, demonstrating that she was not afraid to experiment and to express. Viewed in the context of her subsequent life, retiring and gentle, her painting reveals an inner energy and strength of vision.
>
> The Corcoran Gallery of Art pays homage to a sensitive painter and dedicated individual who through her painting and patronage was much involved in art.
>
> Even today, fifty years since they were stored away, the paintings are strong and vital, refreshing and rewarding in the clarity of expressive imagery. This turn-of-the-century American woman shows a sensitivity and accomplishment that are worthy of recognition. The paintings are only a part of that recognition; the great Reeves Collection also pays tribute to her sensibility and understanding. In the context of her time, the paintings of Louise Herreshoff remain fresh and vibrant still,

bringing to the viewer the inner energy inherent in a dedicated and devoted painter.

Norman Hirschl wrote:

With the great renaissance in American painting now being experienced throughout the nation (and with exhibitions abroad as well), there is a rush to discover and rediscover the forgotten and neglected artists of our past. But too often the yardstick of quality is set aside in an effort to revive a local "also ran."

How rare it is, then, to find a relatively little-known artist whose work is characterized by her singular devotion to inspired painting. Such is the example of Louise Herreshoff.

It was my unique experience to see the fascinating gamut of this artist's work brought out into the sunshine from a dark storeroom at Washington and Lee University.

In my opinion, Herreshoff, an American artist, meets the criterion of quality.

Two of Louise Herreshoff's earliest portraits have the introspective solidity of Sargent and Chase, painting in 1897: *Miss T (Girl With Violets)* and *Portrait of Miss Edith Howe*. And look now at the slashing blocking-out of the characterful *Portrait of My Aunt Elizabeth* of 1926. Between these dates are beach scenes and flowers that might well have been exhibited next to the best of the Expressionists in the Armory Show of 1913.

With Louise Herreshoff, we truly have a new name to add to the growing list of contributors to America's preeminence in the field of twentieth-century art.

CHAPTER

15

A ROAN ANTELOPE?

The parents' deep interest and knowledge of ceramics was soon apparent as I watched them, in that crowded basement, unpack and admire piece after piece in the Reeves Collection of porcelain. I was unsure of what their reaction would be to the art of Louise Herreshoff.

With two sons at Washington and Lee, they were visiting the university for a dinner honoring major donors, known as Lee Associates. Something during our dinner conversation had led the conversation to the Reeves Collection. It usually did. I asked, casually, if they would like to visit the basement where the objects were stored. They agreed. We were in the crowded cellar until after midnight.

The next day they saw the Herreshoff paintings hanging on the chicken wire. Their curiosity was more than casual. The father had graduated from the Virginia Military Institute, just next door to the university in Lexington. I would learn, too, that they were collectors of big game trophies, western sculpture and Impressionist paintings.

During the course of dinner the night before, I had mentioned a project under way at the Student Union building to house an informal gathering place for students and their dates, to be known as the Cockpit. My comment sparked an unusual offer.

"Would you like one of our game trophies — a mounted head of an African roan antelope — for the wall?" he offered."Perfect!" I accepted, having never heard of a roan antelope, much less seen one.

"Great. I'll have my son bring it to you from his next trip home."

And he did. Looking out of my office window on the first floor of Washington Hall one Monday morning, I saw a large plastic wrapped object approaching the building. The package obscured the deliverer, but I could clearly make out long horns and fur, all being carried gingerly across the Colonnade. The trophy, in the eyes of a game hunter, was magnificent. Until the Student Union was completed, the head hung behind my desk. A conversation piece? Yes, but more importantly it was the beginning of a personal and professional friendship with the parents, their sons and the antelope.

Washington and Lee's president, Robert Huntley, had specifically forbidden me from soliciting funds to house the Reeves Collection from sources that might be potential prospects for the university's upcoming capital campaign. Knowing this, I asked him if I might approach the couple who gave the antelope trophy.

"Sure, go ahead," the president replied. "They've said 'no' to our new Commerce School and the proposed new library, and I doubt they'll give to your project. But good luck."

Col Alto, which was a mile from the campus, had since proven too expensive to restore. I now had in mind a project involving one of four 1840s faculty residences that frame the Colonnade on the university's historic front campus. The Greek revival house of red brick with white columns would be the perfect setting for research and exhibition of the Reeves Collection of porcelain and paintings. The eight-room house with an unfinished basement was smaller than Col Alto, but the location was ideal for attracting students and visitors.

THE REEVES CENTER,
WASHINGTON AND LEE UNIVERSITY

An addition of a sunken gallery at the rear would permit the Herreshoff paintings to be properly displayed. Students would also be able to use the space to meet, have lunch, report on projects selected from a "need-to-do list" and hear guest lecturers.

A meeting between Celeste and me with the prospective donors was arranged at their summer home at Virginia Beach. A cardboard mockup of the house at 30 University Place explained the anticipated program and the estimated cost: $500,000.

Within a week, the couple called to say "yes." Work began immediately. The collection had a home, and, in time, the home had students, scholars and visitors from across the country and around the world.

These two generous donors would later open their own expansive home on the banks of the James River and company offices of Ethyl Corporation in Richmond, Virginia, to Reeves Center students. They traveled with the students by bus, van and airplane to visit collections in private hands and public museums around the country. They were an integral part of the Reeves Center's development both financially and inspirationally. In addition to restoring the house, they would endow the directorship and establish funds to be applied to its program.

Elisabeth Shelton Gottwald and Floyd Dewey Gottwald Jr. had helped unpack the porcelain; they offered to have an exhibition in their home of the Herreshoff paintings for alumni; they restored a historic house for research and exhibition of a collection, established endowments; they worked and traveled with the Center's students.

CHAPTER

16

NEW BEGINNING

Working with the architects and contractors on the restoration of the Greek revival house, built for about $3,500 in the 1840s, opened a new chapter in a learning experience that had begun in Providence, Rhode Island, in February 1964. The building, except for the gallery, would retain its original configuration. The interior display would follow as closely as possible the dream of Boy as he had planned in his mind the placement of the collection in Col Alto.

The restoration was completed, and the Reeves Center for the Research and Exhibition of Porcelain and Paintings opened in September 1982 with the annual meeting of the Decorative Arts Trust, a national organization devoted to the study of decorative and fine arts. More than 240 members from twenty-five states and England would spend three days on the campus to hear speakers on various aspects of the eighteenth-century Chinese trade with emphasis on the export porcelain. The Reeves Collection would serve as the resource for a "hands-on" experience.

With Wendall Garrett, editor of *The Magazine Antiques* of New York, and John A. H. Sweeney of Delaware's Winterthur Museum as program directors, the professional tone was set for the theme, "Cross Currents of the China Trade."

The panel of speakers and scholars included Dr. Clare Le Corbeiller and Carl Dauterman of the Metropolitan Museum of Art, New York; Mrs. Jennifer F. Goldsborough of the Maryland Historical Society in Baltimore; Carl L. Crossman of Childs Gallery, Boston; Mr. and Mrs. William J. Flather III of Washington, D.C.; Dr. John Q. Feller of Scranton University in Scranton, Pennsylvania; David Sanctury Howard from London; Dr. H. A. Crosby Forbes of the China Trade Museum in Milton, Massachusetts; Ross E. Taggart from the Nelson Gallery in Kansas City, Missouri; Margaret Klapthor from the Smithsonian Institution in Washington, an authority on presidential items; Donald Gonzales of Colonial Williamsburg; Joella and Stewart Morris of the Museum of Southern History in Houston; Marion S. Carson of Philadelphia; Jack W. Warner of Tuscaloosa Alabama; Dewey Lee Curtis, a founding member of the Decorative Arts Trust from Pennsbury Manor, Pennsylvania; Professor I-Hsiung Ju of Washington and Lee; Royster Lyle and Professor Pamela Simpson, both architectural historians in Lexington, Virginia; and the couple who made possible the restoration of the historic house as a working repository for the Reeves Collection of porcelain and paintings, Elisabeth and Floyd Gottwald.

With the endorsement of America's leading scholars of the China trade, the Reeves Center received considerable national attention. At the beginning, the student body it served was all-male, but fortunately attracting young men became easier as students from nearby women's colleges such as Hollins, Sweet Briar and Mary Baldwin joined their Washington and Lee counterparts on independent study projects in the Reeves Center.

Ben Chapman, a Washington and Lee alumnus, joined my associate James Kirkland and me as our "dollar-a-year" man. (Incidentally, he was never paid.) No task was impossible for these men: Mr. Kirkland, a retired U.S. Army sergeant, and Mr.

Chapman, a direct descendant of owners of nineteenth-century clipper ships plowing the oceans to and from China.

Interest among the Center's students and its director in the history of ceramics and paintings would take them singly or together on short and long segments by land, air and sea around the world. A large portion of the students' travel expenses were met by Janet and Arlen Cotter of Columbia, South Carolina, and Elizabeth and Jack Warner of Tuscaloosa, Alabama.

At Thursday lunches in the Elisabeth Shelton Gottwald Gallery, students would report informally on their various trips and ways in which the Reeves Center inspired them in directions beyond the Center's walls. Required public speaking before classmates and acting as guides to visitors soon turned freshman shyness into confidence.

In some instances, students who had traveled to Asia would report on their trips along the China Sea and the Pearl River, past junks and pagodas, past Whampoa, the anchoring point for foreign ships and for the American seamen in the late 1780s.

In 1987 Louise Herreshoff gained more national attention, equaling that from her one-woman show at the Corcoran Gallery of Art. Her still life, *Poppies,* was selected as one of 125 works of art created by American women artists ion the century between 1830 and 1930, for the inaugural exhibition at the National Museum of Women in the Arts in Washington, the first museum in the world devoted to female artists. The museum was the achievement of Wilhelmina Holladay, who, as a collector, spearheaded the drive that brought to fruition her dream of recognition for women artists. Sixty-seven years after *Poppies* was painted and twenty years after a wet cloth wiped four decades of dust from the glass and produced an explosion of color, Louise would hang with the best. The painting, strong and bold, held its own brilliantly hanging next to Georgia O'Keeffe's *White Trumpet Flower* in the new museum.

Roberta Smith, art critic for the *New York Times*, would report, "Another work that makes one curious to see more is the roughly impastoed painting of flowers by an artist named Louise Herreshoff (1876-1967)."

Three years later, art historian William H. Gerdts would write in his two-volume work, *Art Across America, Two Centuries of Regional Painting — 1710-1920:*

Louise Herreshoff grew up in Providence and studied from about 1890 through 1902 in France, with a short interruption back in Providence in 1896-98. Her French paintings are remarkably evocative, poetic renderings of women. Even more astounding, however, is the work she began to do when she returned to Providence in 1911, after almost a decade in New York City. In the figures, landscapes, and especially the floral still lifes she painted, Herreshoff adopted a blazing palette of unmodulated colors applied in thick brush strokes. The results recall the works of Fauves such as Henri Matisse and certainly mark her not only as the most avant-garde of Providence artists, but as a leader of Post-Impressionism in America.

"A leader of Post-Impressionism in America." Could we — or she—have asked for more?

From behind the front door of an unpretentious, weather-stained, wood-shingled house on a snowy, icy day, a world would open to bring recognition of Louise Herreshoff, an American artist discovered; the establishment of the Reeves Center for the Research and Exhibition of Porcelain and Paintings with the Herbert G. McKay Library; the Marian Carson Collection of George Washington prints; the restoration of the Joella and Stewart Morris Guest House on the university's historic front campus; the John G. Hamilton Program Fund; the construction of the Watson Pavilion for Asian Art; the Jacob J. and Bernice Weinstein Collection of Contemporary Art; supporting endowments for each; and, most importantly, the collection's availability to students and scholars as an international asset of Washington and Lee University. It all began with a penny postcard from a long-forgotten alumnus asking:

"Someday I may wish to make a donation of a work of art to the university. Are you interested?"

NEW BEGINNING

DOL AND BOY NEARING THEIR SILVER WEDDING ANNIVERSARY, 1966

FRONT DOOR TO THE "LITTLE MUSEUM" WITH YALE LOCKS,
93 BENEVOLENT STREET

ACKNOWLEDGMENTS

At various times in varied ways, known and unknown, many individuals stepped with me in February 1964 through the threshold of 93 Benevolent Street in Providence, Rhode Island. The heavy door had guarded for years the treasures of decorative and fine arts within, which were to become the foundation of the Reeves Center at Washington and Lee University.

The educational mission the Center serves is a result of the special contribution each has made. Undoubtedly, my more-than-eighty years have confounded my best intentions; I surely have omitted names that rightfully belong on this long list of individuals to whom I am gratefully indebted.

Scaisbrooke Abbot
Cameron Adams
Mr. & Mrs. Frank Adams
Betsy & Peter Agelesto
Linda Agnor
Hope Alexander
Susan M. Alsop
American Ceramic Circle
Beulah Anderson
Helen & Thomas Anderson
Stephen Andrews
Laura & David Anthony
Virginia Reeves Apple
Katherine & Hunter Applewhite
Dan Arje

Vivian & Michael Arpad
James Arthur
Ellie Atuk
Catherine McCullough Austin
John Austin
John Ayers
Glenn Azuma
Holly & Charles Bailey
Nat Baker
Letitia Baldrige
Tom Bane
Carlotta & Danielle Barker
Mr. & Mrs. Waller Barrett
Stanley Barrows
Dean C. Barry

Kelly L. Bass

Lauren Batte

Trixie & Upton Beall

Patricia Beard

Theodore Beckhardt

William Beiswanger

Spencer Bell

Adrian Bendheim, Sr.

Ralph Benson

Mr. & Mrs. Robert Bentley

Zinkie & Fox Benton

Ally & Art Birney

Octavia & Joe Birnie

Joyce & Ed Bishop

Julia Bissell

Betty Bivins

Levi Bivins

William Bivins

Mr. & Mrs. Daniel Blaine

Bill Boardman

Elisabeth & Laurent Boetsch

Mary Morris & Lea Booth

Mary Booton

Dr. and Mrs. Chris Bosworth

Mary Lee Bowman

Mr. & Mrs. Thomas Bradshaw

Mary & Pat Brady

Trudi & Tom Branch

Adelyn Breeskin

Patrick Brennan

Robert Brennan

Timothy Brennan

Irving Bricken

Libby & Tom Broadus

Ellen & Frank Brooks

Barbara Brown

Henry Brown

James W. Brown

Maria Brown

Robert G. Brown

Sheila Brown-Brown

Michelle Bryan

Marion Bryant

Matthew Bryant

T.B. Bryant

Phillip Budrose

Carter Burgess

Koren Washington Burgin

Pamela & Tom Burish

Michael Burke

Dennis Burnside

Floyd Buxton

Mayrene & Stewart Buxton

Cabell Foundation

Mr. & Mrs. Phillip Caldwell

Bessie & Carl Camper

Elisabeth Carson

Marian Carson

Alfred Carter

John Carter

Samuel Carter III

Jean & Preston Caruthers

Linda & Gray Castle

Jane Cavanaugh

Karrie & Christopher Cerone

George Chang

Luke Chang

Pat & Ben Chapman

ACKNOWLEDGMENTS

Jeanna & Robert Chapman
Mary Tyler & Leslie Cheek
Christopher Chenery
Mrs. Frazier Cheston
Jerry Clark
Mary Louise & Hal Clarke
Agnes Cliff
Mrs. Maurice Cline
Judy & Fred Coffey
Ann Cook Cole
Lois & Fred Cole
Matthew Cole
Gray Coleman
Maria & Milton Colvin
Betty & Chris Compton
Clement Conger
Cathy Barger Conrad
Betty Jo Cook
Rodney Cook
Pamela Copeland
Shawn Copeland
Caroline Cole Cornwell
Mr. & Mrs. Alan M. Corwin
Mary & Sydney Coulling
Janet & Arlen Cotter
Tom Courtenay
The Baroness Cox
Fred Cox
Ann & B.W. Crain
Lacy Crain
Rogers Crain
Mary Spencer & George
Craddock
Suzanne & Jack Crist

Skip Cross
Carl Crossman
Walter P. Chrysler
Marian Culpepper
Alice Cunningham
Helen Cunningham
Mr. & Mrs. John Curtis
John Cushion
Mr. & Mrs. Ralph Cusick
Gov. & Mrs. John Dalton
Gerald Darrell
Burr Datz
Martha Daura
Pierre Daura
Erin Walsh Daunic
Carl Dauterman
Coco Davis
Mr. & Mrs. Garland T. Davis
James Davis
Roger Day
Ambassador & Mrs. John G. Dean
Anthony du Boulay
Decorative Arts Trust
Donald Delahunt
Robert de Maria
Frances Denny
Martha Lou & Buddy Derrick
Albert Dervaes Family
Arthur S. Dervaes Family
Doris & Paul Dervaes
Lisette & Jules Dervaes
Susan Gray Detwiler
Louise DeWolf
Family of Ramdoolal Dey

Wilton Dillon

Lloyd Dobyins

Gary Dobbs, Jr.

Gary Dobbs, Sr.

Harry Dobson

Virginia & Francis Drake

Frances Reeves Drayton

Graham Drayton

Dufy & Bev duBose, Jr.

Elizabeth duBose

Eileen & Bev duBose III

Lee Dudley

Letty & Waller Dudley

Charles Dunn

Harry F. duPont

Jesse Ball duPont

Joei Dyes

Barry Eckert

Callie & Ray Efird

Elaine & Tom Ellis

Mimi & John Elrod

Elaine B. Emerson

Hanna Davis Emig

Nancy & Stewart Epley

Jorge Estrada

Jonathon Fairbanks

Catherine Farnham

James Farquhar

Mr. & Mrs. Allen Ferguson

William Fine

William Fishback

Sybil & Robet Fishburn

John Q. Feller

Hortense Feldblum

Nancy & James Flather III

Kirk Follo

English & John Folsom

H.A. Crosby Forbes

Benson Ford

Mrs. Gerald Ford

Foreign Advisory, Inc.

Walton Eagan Foster

E. & J. Frankel

Mrs. John R. Frazier

Alice Cooney Frelinhuysen

Mrs. David Freudenthal

Pat & Tom Frost

Mrs. Marshall Fulton

Robert Fure

Jefferson Davis Futch

Joan & James Gallivan

Joe Galloway

Homer Gamble

Charlotte & Robert Gammon

Louise Garrett

Wendall Garrett

Catherine & Tim Gaylard

Sadie D. & Frank Gaines

William Gerdts

Louise & Frank Gilliam

Agnes Gilmore

Joseph M. Glickstein

Carter Stubbs Goad

Patrick Gochar

James Godfrey

Gov. & Mrs. Mills Godwin

Brown Goehring

Jennifer Goldsborough

ACKNOWLEDGMENTS

Donald Gonzales
Richard Gooch
Sarah Goodwin
Mr. & Mrs. Dan Gordan
Horace & Eleanor Gordon
Jason Gordon
Rose & Al Gordon
Mr. & Mrs. Aronson Gorman
Chris Gorman
Peter Goss
Scott Gosselink
Connie & Bill Gottwald
Elisabeth & Floyd D. Gottwald, Jr.
Mr. & Mrs. Floyd D. Gottwald, Sr.
Meg & John Gottwald
Henry Grady
Clark Graff
Edward Graves
Zoi & Thomas Graves
David Gray
Gladys Gray
Gus Graydon
Janet Green
Sarah Grier
Helen C. Griffith
Julie & Peter Grover
Mr. & Mrs. William M. Grover, Jr.
Louise Pemberton Guerry
Winifred & Fred Hadsel
Elizabeth Ham
Edward Hamer
Cass & John G. Hamilton
Everett Hamilton, Jr.
Alice & Wilson Hance

Mr. & Mrs. Joseph Handley
Taylor Harbison
Jamie Lee Hardy
Mrs. Phillip Hardy
Randolph Hare
Cynthia & John Harper
Margareta Harper
Betty Harris
Paige Harris
Peyton & Andrew Hart
Houston H. Harte
Clyde Hartless
Norine & Richard Haynes
Frances Schewel Heiner
June & Joe Hennage
Mr. & Mrs. George W. Herndon
Howard Herndon
Richard Herndon
Judith Hernstadt
Charles F. Herreshoff
Dr. & Mrs. David Herreshoff
Freida Herreshoff
James Herreshoff, III
Natalie Herreshoff
Norman Herreshoff
Jane Heyward
Sean Hickey
Jack Hickman
Charles Hilburn
Robert Hileman
Mary Wilson Hilliard
Anita Hinckley
Patrick Hinely
Pruit Hirsch

Norman Hirschl

Nancy & Omer Hirst

Director Ho

Meredith Walker Hodges

Leo & Doris Hodroff

Elise & Henry Clay Hofheimer, II

Wilhelmina Holladay

Betsy & Vernon Holleman

Jane & Sam Hollis

David Hollis

Don Holt

Gov. & Mrs. Linwood Holton

Neil Horstman

Judy & Farris Hotchkiss

Harriet & Royce Hough

Angela & David Sanctuary Howard

Mrs. James Howe

Mr. & Mrs. Les Hudson

Harriet Huger

Shirley & Cyrus Hui

Penny & John Hunt

H. Robert Huntley

Evelyn & Robert E.R. Huntley

J.A. Lloyd Hyde

Mr. and Mrs. Carl Humelsine

Viola & Lowell Humpries

Nancy Iliff

Iliad, Inc.

Dan Ingals

Connie & Bill Ingles

Keith Irvine

Sydney Isenberg

Don Jackson

Marshall Jarrett

Roger Jeans

Jane & William Jenks

Thomas Jenks

John Jennings

Annette & Lewis John

Mr. & Mrs. John Bouvier Johnson

Alex Jones

Bonnie Jones

Dan Jordan

Chowsoon & I-Hsiung Ju

Marion Junkin

Patsy Junkin

Linda & George Kaufman

Mrs. Harry M. Kechijian

Peter Keefe

Robert Keefe

Polly & Chris Keller

Eileen Kelly

Ian Kennedy

Stephen Kent, Jr.

Margaret & James Kirkland

Margaret Klapthor

Cindy & John Klinedienst

Arthur Klyberg

Russell Knudson

Mr. & Mrs. Ira Koger

Ray Kooi

Mimi & S.L. Kopald

Mr. & Mrs. Eugene M. Kramer

Mr. & Mrs. Shelly Krasnow

Angelika Kuettner

Mrs. Russell Ladd

Ruth Lama

ACKNOWLEDGMENTS

Lura & Joseph L. Lanier
Arthur Lans
Patricia Larew
Louise & Bill Latture
Rupert Latture
Linda & C. King Laughlin, II
C. King Laughlin, III
Clare Le Corbeiller
Carew & Robert E. Lee, IV
Christopher Lee
Tom Lee, Jr.
Pat & Gordon Leggett
Powell Leitch, III
Barbara & Bill Lemon
Marguerite & Gerry Lenfest
Mr. & Mrs. Robert F. Levin
Betty & Dan Lewis
Frances & Sydney Lewis
Stanley Lewis
Thomas V. Litzenburg, Jr.
Andrew Logan
Joe Lombardi
The London Symphony
Ann Lothery
Julia & Albert Love
Suzanne Lucas
Mrs. George Lupton
Joseph T. Lykes, Sr.
Marjorie & Joe Lykes, Jr.
Royster Lyle
Mr. & Mrs. Carlyle Lynch
Catherine Lynn
Harry Lyons
Eve & George Macheras

Mrs. Otto Madlender
Richard Madlender
Millie Manheim
Sally Mann
Heather & Hardin Marion
Mary Lynn & Stephen Marks
Blair & David Martin
Christine & James Martin
Ellen Martin
Ramsey Martin
Louise Masson
Annie Massie
Joseph Matthews
Earl Mattingly
Robert McAhren
Mr. & Mrs. Bolton McBryde
Kitty & Bill McClintock
Miriam McClure
Lucille & Stewart McCorkle
Scott McCoy
Cathy McCullough
Timothy McCune
John McDaniel
David McDowell
Terri McFarland
Isabelle McIlvain
Nancy & Herbert G. McKay
Lewis McMurran
Henry McNeil
Robert McNeil
Sue Ann & Otis Mead
Christine Meadows
Branko Medenica
Ronn Mercer

Vera Merchant
David Meschutt
Groke Mickey
Isabelle Middleton
Jefferson Miller, III
Mike Miller
Eleanor & Ross Millhiser
Jeremy Milling
Kaoruko Miyakuni
Wayne Moeller
Dorothy & William Mohler
Suny Monk
Eleanor & Clifford Monohan
Hugh Montgomery
H. Moog
Kenneth Moore
Edward Morris
Joella & Stewart Morris
Joy & Stewart Morris, Jr.
Mrs. Maurice Morris
Vaughan Morrisette
Kevin Morrison
Marion & Robert L. Morrison
Mildred Mottahedeh
Mount Vernon Ladies Assoc.
Jean & Edwin Moyer
Roger Mudd
Steven Mueller
Jean Mudge
Susan & John Mullin, III
Betty & Robert Munger
Charles Murray
Amy Myers
National Preservation Trust

Elizabeth Navarro
David Nave
Peter Neal
Susie & Joe Neikirk
Lowell Nesbitt
William Noel
Woody & Milburn Noel
Larry Norford
Oliver North
Pat & Marshall Nuckols
Jacque & Buck Ogilvie
Marguerite & Bill Old
Joan O'Mara
Kathleen Painter
Sue & George Palmer
Ruth Parmly
Frank Parsons
Mary Raine & Matt Paxton
Catherine & Joseph Payne
Judy Payne
Mr. & Mrs. Howard Peabody
Gwinn Peeper
Harry Pemberton
Robert C. Peniston
Bruce Perkins
Mr. & Mrs. Howard Perkins
Lewis Perkins
Ellen & Marvin Perry
Mrs. F. Bradley Peyton, III
Anne & Tobias Philbin
Dorothy Phillips
Edward Pilley
Mrs. George Pinkley
Coleen Piranian

ACKNOWLEDGMENTS

Marjorie Platou

Louise Platt

Mr. & Mrs. Theodore Plowden

Mr. & Mrs. Francis Plowman

Marjorie Poindexter

Mary Jane Pool

John Pope

Brad Powell

Jo & Lewis Powell

James Powers

Tim Priddy

Roy Prohaska

Laura Purcell

Diana Pusey

Mary Hope & William Pusey, III

Bud Quimby

William Rasmussen

Samuel Rader

Frances Raine

Nancy Raine

Freida Moore Raley

Edna Rand

Bill Raschal

Albertina Ravenhorst

Henry Ravenhorst

Helen Scott Reed

James Rees

Dr. & Mrs. Alex Reeves, Sr.

Alexander Reeves, Jr.

Hazard Reeves

Linda & Chester Reeves

Fannie & W.R. Reeves

Lydia Reid

Helen Sample Rickenbacker

Bruin Richardson

John Riordan

Gov. & Mrs. Charles Robb

Jack Roberson

Letitia Roberts

Ellen & John Robinson

Kenneth Rockwell

Dr. Anne-Imelda Rodice

Felicia Warburg Rogan

Ann Rogers

Lila Rogers

Rodney Rogers

Ross Rosazza

Betsy & Parke Rouse

Charlotte Ruley

Beatrix Rumford

Kenneth P. and Kimberley Ruscio

Preston Russell

Robert S. Ryan

Harold & Israel Sack

Pierre Sagnet

Elaine & Edwin St. Vincent

James Sanders

Lea Santamaria

Vincent Sardi

William Sargent

Chris Schramm

Rosel & Elliott Schewel

Claudia & Fred Schwab

Joan & Isadore Scott

Mr. & Mrs. Stanley DeForrest Scott

Walter Scott

Mary & Willard Scott

William Seale

Mary Holmes & Leon Sensabaugh

Sally & Dick Sessoms

Dr. & Mrs. George Shackleford

John Shank

Baxter Sharp

Gordon Shaw

Cordelia Sherere

Peter Sherwin

Keith Shillington

Linda Simmons

Lisa & Jerry Simon

Pam & Henry Simpson

Roy Slade

Nannette & Stephen Sloan

Albert Small

Buford Smith

Edward Smith

Mrs. Isaac Smith, Sr.

Jane Smith

Marie & Bev Smith

Mason Smith

Rob Smith

Roberta Smith

Stuart & Isaac Smith, Jr.

Famie Smothers

Mary Jane & Vernon Snyder

Jerry South

Southern National Bank

Arlan Spector

Barbara & Ed Spevack

Gordon Spice

Nadine Staton

Janet & Houston St. Clair

Joan Stein

Ruth & John Stemmons

Buford Stephenson

Henry Stern

Peggy & Guy Steuart, II

Stewart Information Services

Amanda Stewart

Robert Stewart

David Hunt Stockwell

Robert Strickland

Jane Stubbs

Sally & Frank Surface

Phillip Suval

John Sweeney

Charles Halfie Swink

Kenneth Swink

Dory Swope

Mrs. Donald Tabutt

John Taffe

Ross Taggart

Betty & Herman Taylor

Elizabeth Taylor

Lee Taylor

Robert Teitelman

Eliza & Bill Thomas

Margaret & Cal Thomas

Nancy & John Newton Thomas

Matthew Thompson

Donald Thayer

Susan Tifft

Lee & Tom Touchton

Betsy & Myron Tremain

Lucille Turner

Robert G. Turner

Cy Twombly

ACKNOWLEDGMENTS

Jane & Allen Tyler
Dorothy & Lewis Tyree
Jon Van Dyke
Susan & Ted Van Leer
The Van Wagenberg Family
Robert Veney
Gretchen Viall
Robert Vienneau
Gudman Vigtel
Virginia Center Creative Arts
Wamsutta Mills
Jessica & Peter Ward
Elizabeth & Jack Warner
Senator John Warner
Thomas Washmon
Elizabeth Otey & William Watson
Helen & William Watt
Louis Watts
Mr. & Mrs. Frank Weatherby
Romulus Weatherman
Michael Webb
Ann Weinstein
Bernice & Jacob J. Weinstein
Lisa Weinstein
Michael Weisbrock
Marjorie & Charles West
Mr. & Mrs. R. J. Whann
Gilles Wheeler
Carson K. Whitehead
Celeste Dervaes Whitehead
James W. Whitehead, Jr.

Elizabeth &
James W. Whitehead, III
Linda & Winston Whitehead
M.K. Key & Paul D. Whitehead
William F. Whitehead Family
Dede & Hal Whiteman
Tony Whitwell
Emily Williams
Marjorie & Ernest Williams
John Wilmerding
Jay Windsor
Anne & John Wilson
Jean & William Wilson
Alice Winchester
Bard Winsley
Meg Winslow
R. Alan Winstead
Bonnie & John Minor Wisdom
Robert Wittpenn
John Wolf
Richard Wolfe
Sheila and Thomas K. Wolfe, Jr.
Mina Woods
James Woodson
Mary & Darryl Woodson
James Woolsey
Elise Hofheimer Wright
Sue & Richard Wright
Bruce Young
Mike Young
Sharon & Harvey Zinn

JAMES W. WHITEHEAD is the retired director of the Reeves Center for the Research and Exhibition of Porcelain and Paintings at Washington and Lee University. During his thirty-five-year career at W&L, he also served as treasurer and secretary to the board of trustees. He graduated from the University of Tampa and served as a naval aviator in the Pacific Theatre during World War II. He lives with Celeste, his wife of 60 years, in Lynchburg, Virginia. They have two sons, James and Paul.